Published by Struik Publishers
(a division of New Holland Publishing
(South Africa) (Pty) Ltd)

Cornelis Struik House
80 McKenzie Street
Cape Town, 8001

86 Edgware Road
London
W2 2EA, United Kingdom

14 Aquatic Drive
Frenchs Forest
NSW 2086, Australia

218 Lake Road
Northcote
Auckland, New Zealand

New Holland Publishing is a member of
Johnnic Communications Ltd

www.struik.co.za

Copyright © in published edition: Struik Publishers 2005
Copyright © in text: Maree Lascaris 2005
Copyright © in illustrations: Louise Lumb 2005
Copyright © in photographs: Bonnie Rodini 2005

All rights reserved. No part of this publication may be reproduced, stored in a retrieval system or transmitted, in any form or by any means, electronic, mechanical, photocopying, recording or otherwise, without the prior written permission of the publishers and the copyright holders.

Publishing Manager: Linda de Villiers
Managing Editor: Cecilia Barfield
Editor: Irma van Wyk
Designer: Louise Lumb
Consulting Designer: Helen Henn
Script: Bonnie Rodini

Reproduction: Louise Lumb
Printing and binding: Paarl Print, Oosterland Street, Paarl

ISBN 1 77007 273 X

1 3 5 7 9 10 8 6 4 2

Log onto our photographic website
for an African experience

Acknowledgements

Maree and Louise would like to acknowledge everyone for their help. If we have left out anyone, please forgive us.

Firstly, to Bonnie Rodini for the concept and for giving us the opportunity to write this book - we would also like to thank her for her work on Tant Sannie's comments. To both our families for their patience and continued support. To Merran Richards for her granny's books, which gave us the inspiration. To Eric Delmont for allowing us to encroach on his privacy in his office at all times of the day and night. To Victoria Goodstein for her patience, company, proofreading and editing. Maree would like to thank Granny Ann, Mutch, Maggie, Olga and Molly for looking after Ben and Lexi when she was unavailable. To my daughters, Lisa and Nicola, for putting up with my bad moods. Louise would like to specially mention her family - thanks to Sally for her research, to Francois for his pictures and to Andrew for all his support with technical and printing knowledge.

And last but not least thank you to Marion Rubidge and Jane and Pete Swartz from Graaf Reinet; Hillary Steven-Jennings from Beaufort West; Sandra Antrobus and her chef, Dalene, from the Victoria Hotel in Craddock; Jonny from Northern Meats; Elma Vertue, Mary van Rensburg, Sugs Smith, Felicity Cooke and Frans from his butchery in Benoni.

Thank you all. Without your help this book wouldn't have been possible.

Tant Sannie

Oven Temperatures

On the farm the best way to test the temperature of the oven is with flour on a baking sheet. Sometimes we use the white paper method.

When testing with flour, sprinkle flour on a baking sheet and place in the oven for 3 minutes –

A very cool oven	the flour will remain white
A cool oven	the flour will be pale yellow
A moderate oven	the flour will be dark yellow
A hot oven	the flour will be light brown
A very hot oven	the flour will be dark brown

When testing with white paper –

A cool oven	paper turns golden brown in 7 minutes
A moderate oven	paper turns golden brown in 5 minutes
A hot oven	paper turns golden brown in 3 minutes
A very hot oven	paper turns golden brown in 1 minute

	Celsius	Fahrenheit	Gas
Very cool	110–120°	225–250°	¼–½
Cool	140–150°	275–300°	1–2
Moderate	160–180°	325–350°	3–4
Moderately hot	190–200°	375–400°	5–6
Hot	220–230°	425–450°	7–8
Very hot	240–250°	475–500°	9

Weights and Measures

Spoons and cups   **Metric equivalent**

1 teaspoon (t)   5 ml
1 dessertspoon (D)   10 ml
1 tablespoon (T)   15 ml
¼ cup (¼ C)   60 ml
½ cup (½ C)   125 ml
⅔ cup (⅔ C)   160 ml
¾ cup (¾ C)   200 ml
1 cup (1 C)   250 ml
4 cups (4 C)   1 litre

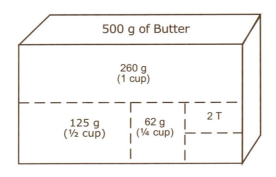

Alcohol Overdose

This remedy comes in useful after big celebrations or weddings. My aunt found this very handy with her husband who liked his brandy too much. In the case of an overdose of laudanum, opium or alcohol, immediately give the person an enema of mustard and water. Most important is to keep the person awake and moving around. Slap them with wet towels and trot them up and down the room until the doctor can be had.

Ant Poison

Those ants are very clever! They always know when we are making chutney or jam. They come out of nowhere!

1 lb brown sugar
1 pint water
6 pence worth of Arsenite of soda

Boil the brown sugar in the water for ½ an hour, let it stand until cold and then add the poison. Stir with a stick and bottle.

Deadly poisonous!!!!!!

MODERN VERSION

As the above poison is no longer sold over the counter, you are advised to go directly to an expert and ask for advice.

Apple Cake

This is a very special treat for us. The apples come from down south and we don't get them that often. They arrived today on the cart but I can't find Lyndall and Em to help me. They are probably at those stupid Bushman paintings! Cream together ½ C butter, 1½ C sugar and 1 C cooked apple pulp. Stir in 1 t bicarbonate of soda and 1 C raisins, stoned. Add butter and sugar, 2 eggs, 1½ C flour, 1 t each of nutmeg, cloves, cinnamon and mixed spice, and a pinch of salt. Bake at 375 °F.

MODERN VERSION

Ingredients

4 large apples, peeled and sliced
½ C water
½ C butter
1½ C sugar
2 eggs
1½ C flour
1 t ground nutmeg
1 t ground cloves
1 t ground cinnamon
pinch of salt
1 t baking powder
1 C raisins or fruit cake mix
icing sugar

Method

Place the apples and water into a pot and boil for about ½ hour until the apples are soft enough to mash. Allow to cool. Cream the butter and sugar; add the cold apple pulp and mix further. Add the eggs, beating well after each addition. Mix in the dry ingredients except the icing sugar. Pour into a well-greased, floured ring mould cake tin. Bake at 180 °C for 45 minutes. Turn out onto a wire rack and allow to cool. Sprinkle with icing sugar, or spread with icing. Cream together 2 T butter, 1 C icing sugar and a few drops vanilla essence. Stir in the cream cheese.

Apple Tart

We have been very busy in the kitchen using all the apples that arrived yesterday. The girls finally came back. I promise I won't give them any of these cakes if they keep disappearing. I know it is that Lyndall! Ingredients: ¼ lb flour, 1 egg yolk, ¼ lb butter or lard, 1 T sugar, pinch of salt and 1 t cinnamon. Rub all the ingredients together and press into a pie dish, keeping enough crumbs to cover the filling. Add the filling and cover with the crumbs. Bake in a moderate oven. For the filling: sweetened apples and raisins.

MODERN VERSION

Ingredients

PASTRY

½ C sugar   1 C butter
1 egg   1 t vanilla essence
2 t baking powder   2 C flour

FILLING

7 tart apples, peeled and sliced   1 t ground cinnamon
3 T flour   1 t lemon juice
½ t ground nutmeg   4 T butter
¾ C sugar

Method

Place all the pastry ingredients into a mixer. When they form a ball remove and press half of the dough into a pie dish, keeping the other half for the top. Spread the apples over the pastry; sprinkle the rest of the ingredients, excluding the butter, over the apples. Break the butter into small pieces and spread evenly. Then cover the apple mixture with small pieces of the remaining pastry. Bake at 180 °C until golden, about 30 minutes.

Apricot Chutney

Ingredients: 6 lbs apricots, 1½ lbs onions, 2½ lbs sugar, 1 T each of cayenne pepper, salt and ground ginger (if using fresh ginger, use 2 T, finely minced), ½ lb raisins and ¾ bottle vinegar. Cook the fruit, onions and sugar together until soft, then add the other ingredients, except the vinegar and cook for 3 minutes. Add the vinegar just before removing the pot from the heat.

MODERN VERSION

Ingredients

3 kg apricots
750 g onions
1.25 kg sugar
1 T cayenne pepper
1 T salt

1 T ground ginger or 2 T minced fresh ginger
250 g raisins
2 C white vinegar

Method

Cook the fruit, onions and sugar together until soft. Add the other ingredients except the vinegar and cook for 3 minutes. Add the vinegar last and once stirred in, remove from the heat. Pour into sterilised bottles.

Apricot Preserve

Allow a pound of sugar for every pound of fruit. Peel and halve the apricots. Boil 2 C sugar with 1 C water. As the syrup comes to the boil drop in the apricots. Boil the fruit until the syrup becomes clear and the fruit tender. Remove the fruit from the syrup and place cut side down in hot jars. Fill the jars with boiling syrup and seal immediately.

MODERN VERSION

Ingredients
10 C sugar, approximately the weight of the peeled fruit
5 C water
2 kg apricots, peeled and halved

Method
Boil the sugar and water in a heavy-bottomed pot. As it comes to the boil, add the fruit. Boil until the syrup becomes clear and the fruit is soft. Place the fruit cut side down into hot jars. Fill the jars to the top with the hot syrup and seal immediately. Any leftover syrup can be used as a sauce with other puddings e.g. hot sponge.

Aloe

Em and Lyndall at the Bushman paintings

Bonaparte Blenkins arrives on the farm

Barley Water

This recipe makes 1 gallon of barley water. Wash 1 lb pearl barley. Place in an enamel or other heavy-bottomed pot. Pour over 1 gallon boiling water. Add the rind of 4 lemons, thinly peeled. Boil for five minutes. Allow the mixture to stand until it is nearly cold. Add the juice of 4 lemons and 1 lb sugar. Stir until the sugar has dissolved. Strain through a muslin cloth and bottle. Store in a cool place.

MODERN VERSION

Ingredients
500 g barley
16 C boiling water
thinly sliced rind and juice of 4 lemons
2 C sugar

Method
Wash the barley and place in a heavy-bottomed pot with the water. Add the rind of the lemons and boil for 5 minutes. Allow the mixture to stand until it is nearly cold. Add the juice of the lemons and the sugar. Stir until the sugar dissolves. Strain through muslin and bottle. Serve well chilled.

Bedsores – Prevention and Remedy

Em's father was in bed for six months before he died. Poor old thing really suffered. Rub the skin with lemon juice and the white of an egg.

Biltong – Home-cured

Biltong is very good for long journeys. Ingredients: 2 packets bicarbonate of soda, 2 C brown sugar, 3 C salt and 1 small t saltpetre. Take about 5 lbs good cuts of venison and cut into strips. Mix the above ingredients together well. Place the meat in a basin, cover with the mixture and sprinkle over a little water. Leave for 24 hours, turning the meat twice, then wash the meat lightly and hang up to dry.

MODERN VERSION

The art of making really 'great' biltong is to cut away as much sinew as possible. Prime cuts such as 'rugstring' sirloin or saddle facilitate this.

Ingredients
Sirloin or saddle, cut into steaks approximately 2½–3 cm thick
coarse salt
white or brown vinegar for sprinkling
1½ litres very hot (not boiling) water
about ⅔ C white or brown vinegar
ground coriander
cayenne pepper
garlic salt

Method
Place the cut meat on a baking tray. Sprinkle with coarse salt quite generously on both sides of the meat. Finger splash white or brown vinegar over both sides and leave to stand for 6–7 hours. Pour the hot water and vinegar into a bowl. Dip in each piece of meat and shake till it stops dripping. This washes off excess salt. Place a wire hook in each piece of meat. Place on a baking tray and season on both sides with the spices. Hang to dry in a well-ventilated area.

We bake twice a week on the farm and both the maids and the girls have to help. As the cost of wood is high, daily baking is out of the question. We bake bread, rusks and cakes for special occasions. It is such a big job as we have to supply everyone on the farm.

Biscuits – Basic

I taught this to the girls the other day. Em is good in the kitchen but I give up on that Lyndall. She will never find a man to marry her! Ingredients: ½ lb butter or lard, 1 C sugar, 1 lb no. 3 meal, ½ C milk, pinch of salt and 1 t bicarbonate of soda dissolved in a little milk. Cream the butter and sugar, then add the meal and milk. Beat. Add the salt and lastly the bicarbonate of soda. Roll the dough and cut into shapes. Place on a baking tray and bake in the bread oven at a moderate heat for 15 minutes.

MODERN VERSION

Ingredients

1 C butter or margarine
½ C sugar
3 C flour
few drops of almond essence

Method

Cream the butter and sugar, then add the flour and essence. Press into a greased pan and bake at 180 °C for 40–45 minutes. Because these biscuits are quite basic, you can divide the dough into three and add different ingredients. Add some cake mix, cinnamon and allspice to one-third; chocolate chips to the second third; and perhaps leave one third plain or even add ginger.

Bobotie

A stranger arrived on the farm today, but I don't trust him. Lyndall can take dinner down to him. I got this recipe from my niece, Trana. She's very rich and can get all the ingredients on her farm easily. Mix 24 dried apricots or peaches, soaked overnight and boiled in a pot until soft and loose, with 4 lbs minced mutton. Add the juice of 2 lemons, 4 T vinegar, 2 D sugar and 4 D curry powder, and mix well. Place the mixture into a pie dish and pour over 2 large C milk into which 4 eggs have been beaten. Stick a few bay or lemon leaves, if available, upright in the meat mixture. Bake in a hot oven for ½ an hour.

MODERN VERSION

Ingredients

1 thick slice of white bread, crusts removed
¾ C milk
2 T oil
2 T butter
2 onions, finely chopped
2 cloves garlic, crushed
1 T curry powder
2 t salt
2 T chutney
1 T apricot jam
1 T Worcestershire sauce
2 t turmeric
2 T brown vinegar
1 kg raw beef mince
¼ C sultanas
3 eggs
pinch each of salt and turmeric
a few bay leaves

Bay leaves

Method

Soak the bread in the milk. Heat the oil and butter in a large pan, then add the onions and garlic and fry. When soft, add the curry powder, salt, chutney, jam, Worcestershire sauce, turmeric and vinegar. Mix well. Squeeze the milk out of the bread and reserve the milk. Add the bread to the pan together with the mince and sultanas. Cook over low heat, stirring until the meat loses its pink colour. Remove from the stove. Allow to cool slightly, then add 1 beaten egg and mix well. Spoon the mixture into a greased baking dish (28 x 16 cm) and level the top. Beat the remaining eggs with the reserved milk (should be about 1⅓ C), add the salt and turmeric. Pour over the meat mixture. Stick a few bay leaves into the meat mixture. Stand the dish in a larger dish containing cold water. Bake, uncovered for 1 hour at 180 °C.

Our national bird: The Blue Crane

Brawn

This is my favourite and everyone knows it! Ingredients: 2 pig's trotters and 4 lbs shin of mutton, salt, pepper, whole cloves, 1 large onion, parsley, thyme, bay leaf and 2 T vinegar. Cover well with water and cook slowly all day. Remove the bones and chop the meat finely. Wet a mould with water, place the meat in the mould and pour the liquid over the meat. Allow to set in a cool place.

MODERN VERSION

Ingredients

2 pig's trotters
2 kg beef shin
1 large onion, chopped
1 bunch parsley, chopped
1 t dried thyme
2 bay leaves
2 T vinegar
salt and black pepper
6 whole cloves
water to cover

Method

Place all the ingredients in a heavy-bottomed pot. Allow to simmer slowly for about 6 hours. A potjie can be used for this recipe although I find it best to do it in a pot in the oven, as nothing sticks. Remove the bones from the meat and cut up finely. Wet moulds or bread tins with water. Place the meat into the moulds or tins and pour the liquid through a muslin cloth over the meat. This should make two loaves. Check the seasoning – the brawn should be slightly over seasoned – then place in the fridge to set. Turn out and serve with a salad.

Bread

We bake this in the oven outside at sunrise and have bread and jam for breakfast. Ingredients: 12 C bread flour, 2 T salt and 2 T sugar. Pour two thirds of the yeast mixture (see Plantjiebrood on page 99) into the dry ingredients. Add enough warm water to make a moist dough. Knead the dough well until it is elastic and easy to handle. Place in a bowl and cover. Keep in a warm place and allow to rise until it has doubled – about 2-3 hours. Knead again and place into greased bread tins. This will make 6 small loaves or 3 long ones. Place in a warm spot and allow the dough to reach the top of the pans. Bake in a hot bread oven and bake for 45 minutes to 1 hour.

MODERN VERSION

Ingredients
12 C bread flour
2 T salt
2 T sugar
4 packets instant yeast
warm water

Method
Mix the dry ingredients together. Stir in the instant yeast. Add enough warm water to make a soft dough. Spoon the mixture into greased, floured bread tins. This will make 6 small loaves or 3 long loaves. Place in the warming drawer and allow to rise for about 30–45 minutes, until the dough reaches the top of the pans. Bake at 200 °C for 45 minutes.

Bredie – Green Bean

Replace the tomatoes in the Tomato Bredie recipe (below) with 2 lbs green beans, sliced. It will need 2 C water. A good addition is 6 potatoes, peeled and chopped, added on the top 1 hour before serving.

Bredie – Pumpkin

This is made the same way as the Tomato Bredie (below). Omit the tomatoes and replace with 4 C pumpkin. Two green peppers are also a good addition to this bredie. Adding cinnamon and nutmeg always works with pumpkin. The pumpkin will be drier than the tomatoes, so add a little stock.

Bredie – Tomato

We eat this nearly every week. It is a stew, made from the fat ribs of mutton and seasonable vegetables. Ingredients: 4 lbs mutton rib, cut into pieces, 2 T lard, 4 onions chopped finely, 16 tomatoes, peeled and cubed, 2 teaspoons salt, 2 t brown sugar and 2 t pepper. Heat the fat in a heavy-bottomed pot on hot coals in the hearth. Brown the meat and set aside. Brown the onions, add the tomatoes and cook for about 10 minutes. Return the meat to the pan, add the seasoning and sugar. Put the lid on the pot, move to a cool spot on the hearth and allow to simmer gently for about 2 hours. Skim the top regularly. Do not add water as the tomatoes should be moist enough. Serve the bredie with rice. Dumplings (see page 29) can be added to absorb some of the gravy.

MODERN VERSION

Ingredients

2 T olive oil	16 tomatoes, peeled and cubed
2 kg mutton rib, cut into pieces	2 t salt
4 onions, finely chopped	2 t pepper
2 cloves garlic, crushed	2 t brown sugar
2 chillies, chopped and seeds removed (optional)	

Method

Heat the oil in a heavy-bottomed pot on top of the stove (a potjie can also be used for this recipe). Brown the meat and set aside. Brown the onions, garlic and chillies, add the tomatoes and cook for about 10 minutes. Return the meat to the pan, add the seasoning and sugar. Put the lid on the pot, place in the oven and allow to simmer gently for about 2 hours. Skim the fat off the top at least twice during the cooking process. Modern tomatoes are not always as moist as they should be, so check the water and add more if dry. However, the tomatoes should be moist enough. Serve the bredie with rice. Dumplings (see page 29) can be added to absorb some of the juice. Bredie can be made with virtually all the seasonable vegetables. I have listed two examples on page 20.

Burns

Equal quantities of raw linseed oil and lime water – excellent for burns. Carbolic oil is another good remedy.

Butter – To keep Cool and Firm

Place the butter in a bowl. Place this bowl in a shallow dish. Purchase an earthenware flowerpot and turn it upside down over the bowl holding the butter. Pour some water, in which some saltpetre and salt have been dissolved, into the dish holding the bowl with the butter. Cover the earthenware pot with a damp cloth, making sure the edges of the cloth are dipped into the water all round. Do not allow the water to overflow into the dish holding the butter. This will keep the butter cool and firm. Place the dish in a draught. Check the water, as it evaporates quickly.

Cabbage Rissoles

I know Lyndall doesn't like this but that girl needs some meat on her bones.
Ingredients: 1 medium cabbage, ½ lb pork mince, ½ lb mutton mince (you could use pork sausage or boerewors), 1 large onion, chopped, a little flour and lard for frying. Wash the cabbage leaves, place into boiling water and allow to boil until soft. Drain. Mix the meat with the onion, shape into 8 rissoles and roll in the flour. Wrap each rissole in a cabbage leaf, making sure you tuck in the edges. Heat the lard in a large, thick-bottomed saucepan, place the rissoles in the saucepan, cover with a lid, lower the heat and allow to simmer gently for 1 hour. Add a little water during cooking when necessary to prevent catching. When ready, the rissoles should be brown on the bottom and moist on the top.

MODERN VERSION

Ingredients
1 cabbage with large leaves, the base of the hard core removed
500 g beef mince
500 g pork mince
1 t salt
good grinding of black pepper
½ t ground cloves
1 T butter
1 egg, beaten
butter to spread on leaves
2 large onions, sliced
oil or dripping
1 C boiling water

cont.

Cabbage Rissoles cont.

Method

Wash the cabbage leaves, place them in a pot of boiling water and allow to cook until they are flaccid (about 5 minutes). Remove and drain. Mix the minced meat, seasoning, butter and egg. Spread each cabbage leaf with a little soft butter and place a roll of the meat mixture on each leaf. Roll the leaves up making sure you tuck in the edges. Fry the onions in a large, flat-bottomed saucepan in the oil or dripping until they are brown. Add the cabbage rolls and allow them to brown slightly. Add the boiling water. Put the lid on the pan and simmer gently for an hour. Check the water during the cooking process, adding more boiling water if necessary. Serve with mash potatoes and sweetened pumpkin.

Our milking cow, Clara-Bell. Trana's family is rich. They have 10 milking cows.

Chicken Pie

Cut up a fowl into small pieces. Put it into a saucepan with some cut up ham or bacon, add 10 whole cloves, cover with water and boil for 15 minutes. Add 3 T lard, salt, pepper and nutmeg. Continue to boil until the meat is tender. Remove the chicken. Mix 3 T flour with a little water to make a smooth paste, add to the juices in the saucepan and allow to thicken. Remove all the bones from the chicken and return to the pan. Line a pie dish with puff pastry, prick a few holes into the dough and bake for 10 minutes in a moderate oven. Put the filling on the base and cover with a pastry lid. Prick the top and bake in a hot oven.

MODERN VERSION

Ingredients

2 chickens
2 chicken stock cubes
2 carrots, sliced
2 onions, chopped
salt and black pepper
water
3 t butter

1 heaped T flour
1¼ C reduced chicken stock
1 C cream
300 g Gruyère cheese, grated
8 sheets phyllo pastry
melted butter

Method

Boil the chickens with the chicken stock cubes, carrots, onions, salt and pepper, and enough water to cover the chickens. When cooked, remove the chickens and reduce the stock by half. Make a white sauce using the butter, flour, stock and cream. De-bone and dice the chicken, then add this and the cheese to the sauce. Lay the phyllo pastry sheets in a greased, rectangular pie dish. Use four of the sheets at the bottom, placing one lengthwise, the next one across, and so on, and buttering between each layer. Place the pie filling on top and use the other 4 sheets of phyllo on top. Butter the top and sprinkle with a few drops of water. Bake at 200 ºC for 35 minutes.

For Constipation!

I love my prickly pears but the problem is it brings on the constipation. Ingredients: ½ lb raisins, ½ lb figs, ½ lb dates and ½ lb prunes. Mince together, then work in 6 pence worth ground senna and 6 pence worth glycerine. Put in a jar. Take ½ teaspoonful at night with a glass of water.

Cough Mixture

Ingredients: yolk of 1 egg, 1 D honey, 1 D glycerine, 1 D olive oil and 1 D lemon juice. Beat up the egg well with the honey, then add the glycerine, olive oil and last of all, the lemon juice. Heat well.

Another Cough Remedy

Ingredients: 4 oz linseed (seed), about 1 inch stick of liquorice and 2 pints water. Boil together the ingredients until half the quantity of liquid remains. Strain and give 1 teaspoon 3 times a day or more if the cough is very bad.

Croup Medicine Recipe – for external use only

Em had croup when she was small and I tell you that child was sick for months. She only got better when Lyndall arrived. Mix together 2 oz olive oil, 1 oz oil of amber, 1 dram oil of cloves and 1 dram creosote. Pour the ingredients into a bottle and shake well. Rub on the patient's chest.

Custard – Soft for Pouring

2 egg yolks, 2 T sugar, pinch of salt, 2 C hot milk and a vanilla pod. Beat the egg yolks with the sugar and salt. Pour the milk and vanilla pod on to this and stir. Put into a double boiler and cook, stirring all the time, until it thickens.

MODERN VERSION – Em's Favourite

Ingredients

2 C milk
½ t vanilla essence
2 egg yolks

3 T sugar
pinch of salt

Method

Heat the milk and vanilla in the top of a double boiler, but do not allow it to boil. Beat the egg yolks, sugar and salt until creamy. Pour the milk over the egg mixture, stir well and return to the double boiler. Stir continually until the mixture thickens. To prevent a skin forming on the top of the custard, cover with a piece of wax paper. This is delicious with tarts, fruit or steamed puddings.

Custard Tart

½ C butter, ½ C sugar, 2 eggs, 2½ C flour, 2 t bicarbonate of soda and a pinch of salt. Cream the butter and sugar together. Whisk the eggs and mix into the butter. Mix the dry ingredients and add gradually to the butter mixture. Roll out the dough very thinly, cut into nine-inch rounds (makes 8 or 9) and keep one of the rounds to crumble on the top of the tart. Bake the rounds in a moderate oven until they are lightly browned. Put the following custard between the layers: 2 eggs, separated, 2 T sugar, 2½ C milk and 2 heaped T flour. No butter. Also add a little vanilla pod. Mix together all the ingredients, except the egg whites. Make the custard; only add the stiffly beaten egg whites last when the custard is cool, before putting between the layers of cake.

cont.

Custard Tart cont.

MODERN VERSION – We could make a Pavlova using the egg whites for the meringue and the yolks for the custard.

Ingredients – MERINGUE BASES

⅔ C egg whites
1 T vinegar
1 C sugar

1 T vanilla essence
⅔ C castor sugar
pinch of baking powder

Method
Beat the egg whites until very stiff. Beat in the vinegar. The mixture must be stiff. Slowly add the sugar and the vanilla essence. Finally fold in the castor sugar and baking powder. This should be enough to make 60 individual meringues or 3 meringue bases, 30 cm in diameter. Line baking sheets with aluminium foil, shiny side up. Pipe on the meringue and bake at 100 °C for about 2 hours or until completely dry.

Ingredients – CUSTARD FILLING

8 jumbo egg yolks
1 C sugar
1 C flour, sifted
1 t vanilla essence

3 C milk, scalded
1 C cream, thickly whipped
a little castor sugar to sweeten the cream
1 punnet strawberries

Method
Cream the egg yolks and sugar until white and creamy. Stir in the flour. Add the vanilla essence to the scalded milk. Pour into the egg mixture. Stir to combine. Pour mixture back into the pot and stir until it boils. Remove from the heat and allow to cool. Assemble the Pavlova at the last minute or the meringues will soften. Layer the meringues one on top of the other and place the custard between the layers. Pipe the sweetened whipped cream on the top and decorate with the strawberries.

Dairy

Otto is the manager of the farm and looks after all the animals, so I watch him very carefully. Once a week the girls have to help churn the butter from the creamy part of the milk. When the first crumbs of butter eventually appear they are gathered into a solid lump then lifted out of the buttermilk, which is preserved as a delicacy. The butter is worked with a wooden spatula until all the fluid is worked out. Add salt and work through again. The girls help 'pound' the butter, which they put into wooden moulds to form butter blocks. These are stored in the coolest part of the house. Bonaparte came to church today and had coffee with me in the front room. Afterwards, when he left, I told the maid to put pure cream in his coffee from now on.

For Dandruff

I grab those girls twice a year and give their heads a good washing. To the yolk of one well-beaten egg, add two T brandy. Apply to the scalp 1 hour before washing.

Dumplings

2 T lard, 2 C flour, 2 t bicarbonate of soda, 1 t salt, pinch of nutmeg and ¾ cup milk. Rub the lard into the dry ingredients. Stir in the milk until you have a loose dough. Spoon onto the top of a stew. Allow 20 minutes to cook.

MODERN VERSION

Ingredients

2 T butter
2 C flour
2 t baking powder
1 t salt
pinch of nutmeg
⅔ C milk

cont.

Dumplings cont.

Method
Rub the butter into the dry ingredients, then add the milk, and a little more if needed. Mix until a soft dough is formed. Spoon into the stew and allow to cook for about 20 minutes.

Dumplings – Apple

Use the suet crust recipe on page 88. 4 large apples, ½ C sugar, ¼ C water, ¼ t ginger, ½ T butter. Roll out enough dough to line and cover a Christmas pudding bowl. Peel and core the apples, and boil with all the other ingredients. Mash, place in the bowl and cover with the suet crust. Cover the top with a cloth tied on with string. Steam for 3 hours. Trana ate three helpings of this the other day – that girl can eat!

MODERN VERSION

Ingredients

Make suet crust (see recipe on page 88)	¾ C sugar
6 pie apples, peeled and sliced	1 t ground cinnamon
2 T flour	1 t lemon juice
½ t ground nutmeg	2 T butter

Method
Line an ovenproof bowl with the suet crust. Toss the apples with all the other ingredients, except the butter. Put into the bowl. Put bits of butter on top. Cover with crust. Tie a cloth over the top of the bowl and steam for 3 hours in a pot of water with a rack at the bottom – the water must not exceed two thirds of the bowl. Check the water level from time to time. Serve with custard or ice cream. Gooseberries or any other fruit can be used instead of apples.

Eggs – Ostrich

1 ostrich egg is equal to 24 hens' eggs.

When the egg is open, it must be used within 24 hours.

If using ostrich eggs instead of hens' eggs for a cake, you must beat them very well – for at least 15 minutes.

If you want to replace hens' eggs in a recipe, beat the ostrich egg well, take 4 T of the egg and add 2 T water and milk mixed together. 2 T of this mixture is equal to one hen's egg.

Otto is in charge of the twelve ostriches we have on the farm. He sends one of the labourers to the pen to collect their eggs as those birds can be vicious.

Ostrich meat has only recently become popular. Previously ostriches were only used for their feathers, skin, eggs and eggshells.

Scrambled Ostrich Eggs

Ingredients

1 ostrich egg
12 T milk and water mixed
    (half milk, half water)
salt
white pepper
butter

Method

Beat the egg, milk and water, and salt and pepper together for about 10 minutes. Heat the butter in a heavy-bottomed pot, pour in the egg mixture. Stir constantly until the mixture sets – do not let it get dry. Serves 12 people.

Hard-boiled Ostrich Egg

Place the egg into cold water, bring the water to the boil and allow it to boil for 1 hour. The yolk is a little dry, so if you are serving the egg sliced, add some raw tomato or homemade tomato sauce. When mashing them, add some butter to the yolk.

Egg Flip

A nourishing drink when you have been working out on the farm in the cold weather. It is also a good way of getting a little food into someone who is recovering from an illness. Boil 2 C wine, 2 C water, 8 T sugar, 1 cinnamon stick and 6 whole cloves. When the sugar has dissolved, remove the mixture from the heat. In another bowl whisk 8 eggs well. Remove the cinnamon stick and the cloves from the boiled mixture, stir into the eggs and serve.

MODERN VERSION – Egg Nog

Ingredients
3 eggs, separated
1 T sugar
¾ C cream
½ C brandy, whisky or rum
a few grains salt
ground nutmeg

Method
Whisk the egg yolks until light, then slowly beat in the sugar, cream and alcohol of your choice. Whip the egg whites and salt until stiff. Fold the egg whites into the other ingredients. Pour into glasses and sprinkle a little nutmeg on top.

Ostrich Chicken

Fig Konfyt – Green

Take 100 green figs and scrape in water until the fur has been removed. Cut them at the large end to allow the water to penetrate. Soak them in salt water (equal salinity to sea water) overnight. Place a weight on top to keep the figs down. Next morning boil in water with a good pinch of bicarbonate of soda and a couple of fig leaves, until the figs are tender (test with a match). When they are soft, remove from the water and drain on a cloth. Prepare the syrup by allowing 7 lbs sugar to 100 figs and ½ pint of water to every lb of sugar. Dissolve the sugar and strain through a sieve lined with muslin. Bring to the boil, add the figs and boil until they become transparent-looking and the syrup thickens. Bottle in airtight containers.

MODERN VERSION

Ingredients
48 firm, well-swollen green figs
4 C sugar
2 cm piece root ginger
juice of 1 lemon
1 C water

Method
Wash the figs well making sure all fur is removed from the skin. Cut a cross in the bottom of each fig and soak in salt water overnight. Place a weight on them so they don't float. Put the sugar, ginger, lemon juice and water into a heavy-bottomed pot and add the figs. Heat and stir constantly until the sugar has dissolved, then simmer gently for 45 minutes. The figs should be transparent and the syrup should set when put on a plate to test. Bottle while still warm in warm, sterilised bottles. These are wonderful served with a good Camembert or Brie.

Francolin – Braised

Clean 6 Francolin and reserve the livers; 3 thick slices bacon fat, parsley, salt, pepper, lard, 3 onions, 6 slices raw ham and 1½ pints chicken stock. Chop the livers; mix with the bacon fat, parsley, salt and pepper. Stuff the birds with this mixture. Heat the lard in an iron pot, fry the onions and ham until soft. Place the birds on top of the onions and ham, then add the stock. Allow to simmer gently for 2-3 hours either on open coals or on the stove until the meat falls off the bones. Remove the bones and any excess fat, return the flesh and stuffing to the pot and serve with mashed sweet potatoes.

Francolin in a Cream Curry Sauce

MODERN RECIPE – from a friend in Graaf Reinet

Ingredients
- 5 or 6 Francolin
- 1 packet mushroom soup
- a little butter
- 1 onion, chopped
- 1 x 750 ml red wine

Method
Roll the whole birds in the mushroom soup and lightly fry in butter. Add the onion and fry for a few minutes. Place in an ovenproof casserole dish. Add the red wine to the frying pan and boil for a few minutes. Add to the birds. Cover the casserole dish either with a lid or foil. Bake at 160 °C for about 3 hours or until the meat easily comes away from the bones. Cut the meat off the bones and chop into bite-size pieces. Discard the wine sauce (I give it to the dogs; they love it).

Curry Sauce

Ingredients

2 T butter
3 t curry powder
1 apple, finely chopped
1 onion, finely chopped
1 x 415 g tin mushroom soup
1 C cream
salt and pepper
paprika

Method

Melt the butter in a saucepan, add the curry powder and sauté the apple and onion until the onion is transparent. Add this to the soup and cream. Add the salt, pepper and paprika to taste. Pour over the de-boned francolin and mix together. When re-heating this dish, be careful not to let it boil as the cream will separate. Also, do not microwave. Serve with yellow or brown rice.

Waldo and Otto

Frikkadel

I sent these down to Otto's cabin today. I am sure Bonaparte will love them. Ingredients: 1 thick slice of bread, boiling water, 1 medium onion, 1 T parsley, 2 lbs minced mutton, salt and pepper to taste, 1 egg and 2 T lard. Put the bread into the boiling water, then squeeze out. Finely chop the onion and the parsley. Mix all the ingredients together, except the lard. Form into round cakes. Place on a baking tray with a little lard on top of each frikkadel. Pour a cup of boiling water around them on the baking tray and bake at 375 °F for about 30 minutes. If you want to make old-fashioned frikkadels, you can use beef instead of mutton. Replace the lard with butter.

MODERN VERSION

Ingredients

- 1 kg veal mince
- 2 T grated onion
- 1 T chopped parsley
- 1 t chopped mint
- 1 C breadcrumbs
- 2 eggs
- 1 T wine vinegar
- ½ t dried oregano
- 2 cloves garlic, crushed
- 2 T hot water
- salt and pepper to taste
- flour for rolling
- 2 T olive oil

Method

Mix all the ingredients together and season to taste. Let the mixture stand for an hour. Shape into balls, roll lightly in the flour and fry in hot oil until browned. Drain and serve at once. Alternatively: use the same recipe for the meatballs, but instead of rolling them in flour, drop them into basic tomato sauce (see page 37). The sauce must be warm. Allow the balls to boil gently for about half an hour. Serve these cold as a snack or hot with rice as a meal. They taste better if re-heated and eaten the day after they are cooked.

TOMATO SAUCE – basic

Ingredients

1½ T olive oil
1 small onion, finely chopped
2 x 410 g tinned tomatoes *or*
16 fresh tomatoes, chopped
2 T tomato puree

2½ t finely chopped basil
½ t salt
black pepper
1 t sugar

Method

Heat the oil, add the onion and cook until soft and transparent, not brown. Add the rest of the ingredients and stir well. Reduce the temperature and simmer gently, only partially covering the pot. Cook for 45 minutes, stirring the mixture regularly.

The Farmhouse

Fruitcake – Koosani

½ lb sugar, ½ lb butter, 3 eggs, 1 lb flour, ½ lb raisins, ½ lb currants, ½ lb sultanas, 1 oz cherries (if available), 1 oz mixed peel, 1 oz almonds, ½ packet all spice, ¼ t each ground cinnamon, nutmeg, mace and ground cloves, 1 t bicarbonate of soda, 1 T honey or treacle and 1 wine glass brandy. Beat the sugar and butter together until creamy. Add the eggs one at a time, beating well, and alternating with a little flour. Add the rest of the flour with the fruit, mixed peel and nuts. Add the spices, bicarbonate of soda and treacle. Pour in the brandy. Place the mixture in a well-greased cake tin and bake in a moderate oven for 1½ to 2 hours.

MODERN VERSION

Ingredients

450 g butter
3 C soft brown sugar
2 x 100 g packets ground almonds
7 eggs, jumbo
3 C flour
1 t salt
2 kg fruitcake mix
200 g box cherries, halved
1 t baking powder
½ C sherry
375 ml (½ x 750 ml) bottle brandy

Method

Cream the butter and sugar, add the almonds and eggs one at a time. Add 2 C flour and the salt. In a separate bowl coat the fruit with 1 C flour. Combine the contents of the two bowls. Stir the baking powder into the sherry. Combine all the ingredients and stir together well. Place the mixture into a 28 cm square tin, greased, floured and lined with greaseproof paper. Bake at 125 °C for 3 hours. Remove the cake from the tin and pour brandy over while still warm. This cake can be baked, iced and eaten on the same day. As long as sufficient brandy is used, it will be moist and delicious.

Ginger Beer

When the Karoo heat is too much, all I can do is sit on the stoep having my feet washed and drinking ginger beer. Ingredients: 1½ oz root ginger, 2½ lbs sugar, 1 packet tartaric acid, 2 t lemon juice and a little zest, a few raisins and 1 C potato yeast. Bruise the ginger and put it with the sugar into 1 gallon cold water, boil for ½ to ¾ hours. Take off the fire and fill up with cold water to make 3 gallons. When almost cold, add the tartaric acid, lemon juice and zest, raisins and yeast. Stir well, cover and leave in a cool place to ferment for 36 to 48 hours, or until the raisins float to the top. Strain, bottle and cork well (tie down). If possible, leave for 2 or 3 days after bottling.

MODERN VERSION

Ingredients
3½ C sugar
9 litres lukewarm water
1 x 10 g packet instant yeast

1½ t tartaric acid
2 t cream of tartar
2 t ground ginger

Method
Dissolve 1 t of sugar in 500 ml of the water and sprinkle the yeast on top. Set aside until it bubbles. Mix the rest of the ingredients into the remaining water, stir and add the yeast mixture. Cover and place in a warm area. Allow to stand for 12 hours. Pour into bottles and screw caps on securely. Leave for at least 3 days before drinking.

Gingerbread – Aunt Molly

Aunt Molly made the best gingerbread in the Karoo. Ingredients: ¾ C butter, ¾ C sugar, 2 eggs, 1 C sour milk, ¼ C treacle, 3 t ground ginger, 3 t cinnamon, ½ t grated nutmeg, 3 C flour and 1 t bicarbonate of soda (mixed with 2 T hot water). Add fruit if desired and 1 wineglass rum. Cream the butter and sugar. Add the eggs and beat well. Add the milk and treacle, then the mixed spices and flour. Dissolve the soda in hot water and add. Bake in a moderate oven for 1 hour.

Gingerbread – Pam

MODERN VERSION

Ingredients

3 C flour
3 t ground ginger
pinch salt
1 C lukewarm water
3 eggs
1 C sugar

2 t mixed spice
1 t baking powder
1 C golden syrup
1 t bicarbonate of soda
¼ C water

Method

Mix everything together and beat for 5 minutes until the mixture has a gloss to it. Bake at 180 °C for 55 minutes. This bread improves when frozen or kept sealed for a few days.

Gingernut Biscuits

This was my Aunt Min's favourite recipe. Ingredients: ¼ lb butter or lard, 1 C treacle, 1 egg, 1 lb flour or meal, 6 oz sugar, 1 t bicarbonate of soda, 1 t mixed spice, 1 t ground ginger and 2 t ground cinnamon. Warm the butter or lard and treacle. Add this and the egg to the dry ingredients. Knead until the dough is firm and you can roll it out thinly. Cut into shapes. Bake in a moderate oven until brown.

MODERN VERSION

Ingredients

½ C butter
½ C golden syrup
1 egg
3½ C flour
¾ C sugar

1 t baking powder
½ t bicarbonate of soda
1 t mixed spice
2 t ground ginger
add 1 or 2 T milk if needed

Method

Put the butter and syrup in a pan and allow the butter to melt. Add this and the egg to the sifted dry ingredients. Mix well until it forms a firm dough. Roll the dough out thinly and cut into shapes. Bake at 180 °C for 10–15 minutes. Use this recipe to make gingerbread men for the children.

Guinea Fowl

I sent the labourers out today to hunt the quinea fowl. Pluck and stuff them with dried apricots (soaked in water overnight) and apples. Season the birds. Heat some lard in a heavy-bottomed pot, roast the birds until they are golden brown all over. Add red or white wine if available or simply add some boiling water. Close the pot and allow the birds to cook until the flesh falls off the bone.

Guinea Fowl in Red Wine

MODERN RECIPE – from my friend in Cradock

Ingredients
2 or 3 guinea fowl
1 packet mushroom soup
1 T butter
1 T olive oil
1 onion, finely chopped
1 x 750 ml bottle of red wine
1 C chicken stock
black pepper, coarsely ground
salt
4 T tomato sauce
dash Worcestershire sauce
1 punnet white button mushrooms, sliced
2 T flour (if necessary)
1 x 250 g packet rindless back bacon, chopped

Method
Roll the whole birds in the mushroom soup and fry lightly in butter and olive oil. Place the birds in an ovenproof casserole dish. Fry the onion, then add the red wine, chicken stock, the rest of the mushroom soup, coarsely ground black pepper, salt, tomato sauce and Worcestershire sauce. Pour liquid over the birds and seal in a casserole dish. Bake at 160 °C or until the meat is tender. Remove from the oven and take all the meat off the bones. Liquidise the sauce until smooth. If the sauce is very thin, add 2 T flour. Add to the guinea fowl meat. Lightly fry the mushrooms and bacon. Add to the meat mixture. Stir well. Sometimes I add 2 t green peppercorns at liquidising stage, as this gives a completely different flavour. Serve with thin ribbon noodles and a salad.

Hare – Roasted

Waldo caught 6 hares today. That boy might be more valuable than I thought. Skin the hare making sure you remove all the under skins. Remove the head and the front legs. Marinade the hare in white wine, carrots, onions, mixed herbs and bay leaves. Cover and place in a cool place for 2 days. Lard the hare well with pork fat. Place in a saucepan with the marinade and the vegetables; add some fresh vegetables, salt and pepper. Cover and bake in a moderate oven for 1½ hours. The meat should be falling off the bones. If it is an old hare it might require a little more time in the oven. Remove the bones and any excess fat from the hare, return the meat to the pan, add 1 pint sour cream, heat and serve. Serve with mashed potatoes, pumpkin and quince jelly.

MODERN VERSION – given to me by an Italian friend

Ingredients

2 saddles of hare
seasoned flour
½ C olive oil
2 large onions, sliced
2 cloves garlic, mashed

2 t sugar
4 bulbs fennel, quartered
1 C chicken stock
1 orange, juice and zest

Method

Dip the saddles into the seasoned flour. Heat the oil in a heavy-bottomed saucepan and brown the saddles. Remove, add the onions and garlic and brown them. Sprinkle over the sugar and stir. Add the fennel. Place the hare saddles on top of the vegetables. Add the stock and orange juice. Bake at 180 °C for 1 hour. Remove the fillets from the bones, slice and place on the vegetables. Decorate with a few fennel leaves and the orange zest finely chopped with a little garlic. The saddles of hare can be replaced by chicken pieces, leave the skin on and follow the same recipe.

Hints

Our horse: Rupert

To make sour milk add 1–1½ T vinegar, and allow to stand until curdled and sour.

To make sour cream add 2 t lemon juice to ½ C cream and allow to stand. It will become thick and sour.

When baking a cake and you find you are short of one egg, replace the egg with 1 T vinegar.

Honey is the best thing on earth. I am eating 10 spoonfuls every day so that I look much younger to Bonaparte.

In the old days no one doubted the purity or the wonderful powers of honey. Indeed, from the earliest recorded times honey was considered the elixir of youth. Honey is a particularly energising food, providing 300 calories per 100 grams. The sugars it contains are completely assimilated by the body, although honey contains hardly any vitamins. In the diet of children especially, honey can take the place of sugar in almost all of its uses. The quality, consistency, aroma and flavour of honey vary according to the type of flowers and trees most widespread in the region where it is gathered.

The oldest and most valued of all sweeteners is honey. Today many of our foods have lost some of their mineral content, so pure honey is much in demand. Purists seek it from sources where they are sure it is unadulterated.

Invalid Care

When Em's father was dying I kept the sick room as uncluttered as possible. It is very important to keep the room spotlessly clean. The room should be well ventilated, but not draughty. Never whisper in a sick room as this will make the patient anxious. Talk audibly, not too loudly. Only talk to the patient if they want to talk, as talking can be very tiring. When sponging to relieve a fever, add a little vinegar to the water. Always sponge away from the head. When sponging a patient tell a story, even if they do not listen it will take their mind off what you are doing. When bringing food to the patient make sure the tray is clean; when they have finished remove the tray immediately.

Invalid Food

Em's father often had a fever. Only liquid food should be given in small quantities, frequently. Food should never be rich or greasy. It must be as nourishing as possible.

Suggested drinks

Barley water – see page 13
Chicken broth
Beef tea, egg added (optional)
Mutton broth

Suggested food

Steamed mutton chops
Sheep's brains
Junket
Milk toast

Irish Stew

Waldo is in charge of the sheep, but I tell you that boy is so lazy if you don't watch him all the time. But he must earn his keep on this farm. We got this recipe from the settlers in 1820. Ingredients: 3 lbs best-end neck of mutton, milk for soaking, 6 lbs potatoes, 1½ lb onions, salt and pepper to taste. Trim the fat off the neck and cut into chops. Beat the chops with the blunt edge of a knife and soak in milk for a few minutes. Peel the potatoes and slice thickly. Peel the onions and cut into thick slices. Place a layer of potatoes at the bottom of a saucepan, then a layer of meat and onions, season and repeat ending with a layer of potatoes on top. Add a pint of water, close the saucepan and cook in a moderate oven for 2½ hours. Do not lift the lid. If cooking on top of the stove, shake the pot occasionally to prevent sticking.

MODERN VERSION

Ingredients
500 g onions, peeled and thickly sliced
500 g carrots, peeled and sliced in thick rings
5 stalks celery, sliced in thick rings
1.5 kg shoulder of lamb, cubed
salt
black pepper
1 kg potatoes, peeled and thickly sliced
1 C chicken stock

Method
In a casserole dish, layer some onions, carrots and celery, then add a layer of meat, season, and add a layer of potatoes. Repeat the layers until the ingredients have all been used. Pour the stock over the ingredients. Close the casserole and cook in the oven at 180 °C for 3 hours.

Jam – Apricot

Trana is arriving today so I put Em and Lyndall to good use making this. First they stone the fruit and chop it up. If you want fine jam, skin the fruit. Add sugar and fruit – pound for pound. Spread the sugar over the fruit and allow it to stand overnight. Next morning, allow to boil over a very slow fire, for about an hour. Add water if necessary. Bottle in jars that have been thoroughly cleaned and allowed to dry in a cool oven for 15 minutes. The next day when the jam has set, cover the tops with white paper that has been dipped in brandy, before you close the jars. You can even add a piece of tissue paper, brushed with the white of an egg – this will dry and become hard and air tight. 15 lbs of fruit will make 18 pots of jam. The kernels can also be added to the jam. They have an almond taste which is good with the apricot. Simply break the stones, remove the kernel, blanch and add to the stewing sugar and fruit.

MODERN VERSION

Ingredients
5 kg sugar
5 kg apricots, stoned and chopped up

Method
Sprinkle the sugar over the chopped fruit and allow to stand overnight. Place the fruit mixture into a thick-bottomed pot and simmer gently, stirring frequently until the juice becomes syrupy when cooled on a plate. This will take about 45 minutes. Pour into sterilised bottles. This should make 12 jars. The kernels can be added as mentioned above.

Jam – Peach

February is a good month to make this jam as there is always a good supply available. Peel and slice 50 peaches. Place the fruit in salt water for a few hours. Rinse and dry. Weigh the peaches. For every pound of fruit allow 1 cup of water and three-quarters of a pound of sugar. Bring the water to the boil, add the fruit and simmer until tender. Add the sugar and allow it to dissolve, stirring all the time. Cook gently until it has the right consistency and the liquid becomes like a sticky jelly when put on a plate. Skim the top if necessary. Pour into hot, sterilised jars, allow the jam to cool and cover the tops either with candle wax or paper dipped in brandy. Cover the jars and store until needed.

MODERN VERSION

1 kg fruit, 1 C water and 750 g sugar. Follow the same method as above.

Bonaparte greets Trana

Jam Tart

Never leave this unattended – Trana will eat the whole pie if I let her. Use rich short-crust pastry to line your plate or pie dish. Mix 4 T peach jam, 2 T ground almonds, 2 T crumbs (preferably cake crumbs) and one egg. Put this mixture onto the short pastry. Bake in a moderate oven for 20 to 25 minutes. Before serving, place some preserved peaches on the top. Serve with custard and some of the peach syrup.

MODERN VERSION

Ingredients

1 C butter
6 T sugar
6 T oil
2 eggs, beaten
1 t vanilla essence
4 C flour
5 T sugar

4 t baking powder
pinch of salt
1 small tin berry or fruit jam
3 T ground almonds
few drops almond essence
berries or fruit for decoration

Method

Cream the butter, sugar and oil. Add the eggs and vanilla essence, then the sifted dry ingredients. Line a pie dish with half the mixture. Mix the berry jam with the almonds and almond essence. Spread this onto the base. Sprinkle the rest of the pastry mixture on top. Bake at 200 °C for 20 minutes. Decorate with berries or fruit.

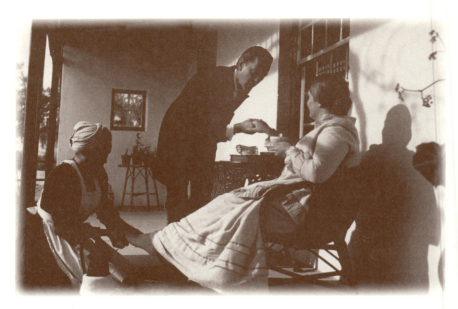

A lekker foot wash. Bonaparte noticed my beautiful feet.

A big meal can make you very tired.

Koeksisters or Koesisters

Koeksisters are rolled out into strips and plaited as the recipe describes. My aunt Sara tells me that the Malay people in Cape Town make what they call a koesister on a Sunday as a treat. It is a slightly spicier version of the koeksister and is made into a ball shape, more like a small vetkoek.

Koeksisters

Syrup: 12 C sugar, 6 C water, 1 T lemon juice, vanilla pod and 1 t cream of tartar. Boil the sugar and water for 8 minutes. Add the lemon juice, vanilla pod and cream of tartar, and boil for 1 minute. Allow to cool. Place the pot of syrup in an earthenware dish filled with cold water. Place in a cool place. Must be well chilled.

Dough: 10 C flour, ½ t salt, ½ lb butter, 3 eggs, beaten, 3½ T yeast, enough water to combine dough and fat for frying. Mix the flour and salt. Rub in the butter, then add the beaten eggs. Spoon in the yeast, add the water and knead for 10 minutes. Roll out the dough on a floured surface, cut with a sharp knife into rectangles — then into 3 strips joined at the top — and plait. Fry in hot, deep fat until golden brown. Dunk into cold syrup for at least a minute. Remove from the syrup and drain. Allow to cool. This makes 15 dozen medium-sized koeksisters. They will keep for months.

The **MODERN VERSION** of this recipe would be almost identical. The ½ lb butter becomes 1 C butter; the yeast is replaced by 3⅓ T baking powder. The syrup is placed into the deep freeze to make sure it is well chilled, not frozen. The koeksisters are fried in hot oil, not fat.

Krengler – this is a recipe given to me by a Danish friend

Trana and I ate lekker Krengler in bed last night. Ingredients: ½ lb flour, ¼ lb butter and 1 C thick cream. Mix into a stiff dough, roll out and cut into strips. Fold into loose knots and dip in sugar. Bake in a moderate oven until the biscuits are golden brown.

MODERN VERSION

Karoo

Ingredients
½ C butter   1 C sour cream
1½ C flour   sugar

Method
Rub the butter into the flour with your fingers. Stir in the cream. This will make a sticky dough. Wrap in wax paper and refrigerate for at least 2 hours. Break the dough into 18 pieces. Roll each piece in sugar until it is like a long snake, long enough to twist and tie into a loose knot. Place onto a baking tray. Bake for about 25 minutes at 180 °C until golden brown. This is excellent dough for Christmas mince pies. Roll out the dough on a floured surface. Cut with a standard glass into circles. Using patty pans, place one circle on the bottom, top with Christmas mince, cover with another piece of dough, seal the edges and bake.

Tant Sannie and Trana

Leg of Mutton

Weigh the leg: the cooking time will be 20 minutes per pound plus an extra 20 minutes. Lard the leg well by threading sheep tail fat through the meat. Cut the fat into small strips and roll in salt and pepper. Cut slits into the leg with a knife and press the strips of fat into the slits. Cut up any seasonal vegetables, such as onions, carrots, turnips and potatoes, and add available herbs. Place them into the bottom of your potjie. Rub the leg with fat and season. Place it into the potjie on top of the vegetables. The meat must be cooked over a slow heat, so be careful not to put too many coals under the pot. Take the leg out of the pot, remove any fat, pour in half a bottle of sweet wine (if not available, use stock) and bring the liquid to the boil. Thicken the liquid with some fat mixed to a paste with flour and stir this in until it thickens. Add quince jelly to taste and check the seasoning. Carve the meat off the leg and return it to the potjie.

MODERN VERSION

Ingredients
1 leg lamb
1 x 250 g packet streaky bacon
olive oil
salt
black pepper
3 large onions, sliced
4 carrots, sliced
2 bunches fresh tarragon
½ T capers
2 t French Dijon mustard
2 T brown sugar
1 jar redcurrant jelly
1 x 750 ml fruity white wine
flour and butter to thicken
1 C cream

cont.

Leg of Mutton cont.

Method

Lard the leg of lamb with the bacon – make slits in the meat and press the bacon in. Rub the lamb with a little olive oil, salt and freshly ground black pepper. Place the vegetables, tarragon, capers, mustard and sugar in the bottom of an ovenproof pot. Place the lamb on top of the vegetables. Close the pot and cook at 220 °C for the first 10 minutes, then drop the temperature to 190 °C for 45 minutes. Uncover the meat. Spread the redcurrant jelly on the top of the leg, reserving half the jar for the sauce, add the wine and allow to cook for a further 45 to 60 minutes. Baste well during cooking. Remove the meat and vegetables from the pan, place on a platter and keep warm in the warming drawer. Remove any excess fat from the pot. Make a paste with the flour and butter, add to the pan juices along with the reserved redcurrant jelly and stir until it thickens. Add the cream, check the seasoning and set aside. Keep warm. Slice the meat, arrange on a platter, surrounded by the vegetables, pour the sauce over the meat and serve.

Waldo bringing the sheep home

Lemon Curd

Ingredients: 2 C butter, 5 C sugar, 2 C preserved lemon juice, 1 T preserved lemon peel and 12 eggs. Melt the butter and sugar in a double boiler, then pour in the lemon juice, rind and eggs. Stir constantly until the mixture thickens. Pour into warm, sterilised jars and allow the curd to cool. Cover the top with candle wax and seal. This should last for several months on the shelf, if stored in a cool place.

MODERN VERSION

Ingredients
2 C butter   juice and rind of 12 lemons
5 C sugar   12 eggs, beaten

Method
Melt the butter and sugar, then add the juice and rind of the lemons, plus the beaten eggs. Stir constantly over a moderate heat until the mixture thickens. Pour into warm, sterilised jars and allow to cool. Screw the lids on tight and store.

Lemon Juice

To preserve lemon juice for future use, you need to clarify the juice. Place the lemon juice into a pot with some egg whites (2 C lemon juice to 1 egg white). Heat gently and do not stir. The heavy sediment will attach itself to the egg white, allowing it to be removed easily. Strain the juice through a cloth, and bottle. Make sure that the cork touches the liquid in the bottle.

Lemon Peel Preserve

Peel as many lemons as you would like to preserve and remove as much white pith as possible. Cut the peel into thin strips, place in a pan of water and bring to the boil. Replace the water and repeat. Remove the peel from the water, allow to cool and weigh. Add the equivalent amount of sugar, cover with water and allow to boil slowly until the peel is transparent and tender. Drain, then toss in sugar. Keep on top of the stove to dry. Toss in sugar again. Store in an airtight jar until needed. Rinse well before using in a recipe.

Lemon Syrup

Grate the rind of 5 large lemons, steep with 1 oz tartaric acid, 3 or 4 C sugar and 5 C cold water. Leave overnight. Next day strain through muslin, and bottle.

MODERN VERSION

Ingredients
8 C lemon juice, strained to remove pips
3 kg sugar

Method
Place the lemon juice and sugar into a double boiler. Heat and gently dissolve the sugar, stirring often. Do not allow to boil. Bottle while hot and allow to cool. Screw on the lids. This will last for months, stored in a cool place. I prefer this recipe as I do not like using preservatives when not necessary.

Light

Candles are made from fat rendered from sheep tails and poured into moulds. When a man comes to visit us, we light a candle and he stays until the candle burns out.

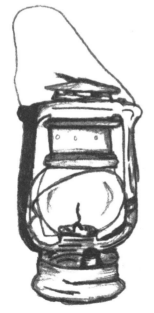

There was great excitement when the first oil lamps came to the farm. Bonaparte caught Waldo taking a lamp into the loft. He was punished for stealing the dried peaches.

Liver Roll

The maid's husband lost our sheep today. If Otto doesn't find them, then they must get off the farm. Mince 1 sheep's liver, 2 slices of bacon fat and 1 onion. Add a cup of breadcrumbs, 1 t salt, 1 t pepper, some grated nutmeg and 2 eggs, lightly beaten. Pour into a greased round tin and steam for 1 hour. This may also be put into a greased ovenproof pot. Stand in a pan of water and bake in a cool oven until firm.

MODERN VERSION – Liver paté

Ingredients
2 eggs
½ C butter
2 x 250 g containers chicken livers
6 rashers streaky bacon
1 onion, sliced
¼ C cream
¼ C brandy
¼ t nutmeg
salt
black pepper
3 T butter, clarified

Method
Place the eggs in cold water. When the water comes to the boil, time 12 minutes. Shell and set aside. Melt 4 T butter and fry the livers, bacon and onion until browned. Place all the ingredients, except the clarified butter, into a liquidiser and liquidise; check the seasoning. Put into a paté dish, cover with clarified butter and serve with toast. To CLARIFY the butter: melt the butter in a pan and when it is melted, pour it through a cloth to remove the sediment.

Locusts – Fried

Plunge the locusts into boiling water; they will die instantly. Pull off the wings and legs. You will be left with the body. Sprinkle salt and pepper over the locusts, drop them into hot fat and fry until crisp. They taste like creamy white bait.

Marmalade – Dried Peach and Lemon

The day Bonaparte got the bad news his wife had died, Lyndall, Em and I were very busy enjoying my new marmalade. Ingredients: 4 lb lemons, 12 pints water, 4 lb dried peaches and 12 lb sugar. Wash the lemons and place in the water in a covered saucepan. Simmer slowly until the lemon skin can be pierced easily – approximately 1 hour. Remove the lemons from the pan, cool and cut up into small pieces. Save the pips, as these are full of pectin. Tie them in a muslin bag. Put the bag back into the liquid and boil for a further 10 minutes. Return the lemon to the liquid with the dried peaches and allow to soak overnight. Remove the bag of pips. Bring the fruit and water to the boil and add the sugar, stirring continually until the sugar has dissolved. Boil rapidly for about 15 minutes and test to see if setting point has been reached. Put into hot, sterilised jars. Allow to cool. Cover securely with paper dipped in brandy, and seal. Store until needed.

MODERN VERSION

Ingredients
500 g lemons   500 g dried peaches
1½ C water   7½ C sugar

Method
Follow the above recipe.

Marmalade - Rhubarb

Trana gave me another marmalade recipe with rhubarb. Whatever will she think of next! Ingredients: 6 lemons, 3 pints water, 6 lb rhubarb and 7 lb sugar. Wash the lemons, place in the water and simmer gently until the skin can be pierced easily. Remove the lemons from the pan, cool and cut up into small pieces. Place the pips in a muslin bag, return to the water and boil for a further 10 minutes. Return the lemon to the liquid and leave overnight. Next day, remove the bag of pips, add the diced rhubarb to the lemon liquid and cook until the rhubarb is tender. Add the sugar and stir constantly until it has dissolved. Allow to boil rapidly until setting point has been reached. Pour into hot, sterilised jars, allow to cool, cover and seal.

MODERN VERSION

Ingredients
3 lemons
1½ C water
1.5 kg rhubarb, diced
7½ C sugar

Method
Follow the above recipe.

rhubarb

Melk Tart

Bonaparte is coming for tea today. This melk tart will make him even sweeter for me. Line three plates with puff pastry (see page 74). Make the following custard: heat 2 C milk with a cinnamon stick in the top of a double boiler. Make a paste with 4 T sugar, 2 T flour and 4 T cold milk. When the milk is hot, add the paste and stir well. Return to the heat, stirring constantly and cook for a further 15 minutes. Remove from the heat and stir in 2 T butter and 2 egg yolks. Leave the mixture to cool. Beat the 2 egg whites until stiff and fold into the cooled mixture. Allow it to get cold before pouring it onto the pastry. Bake at 450 °F for 20 minutes. Sprinkle with cinnamon when you remove the plates from the oven.

MODERN VERSION

Ingredients

PASTRY

- 1½ C flour
- pinch salt
- ⅔ C sugar
- 2 t baking powder
- ½ C butter
- 1 egg
- 1 T milk

FILLING

- 3 jumbo eggs
- 5 T sugar
- 1 T flour
- 3 T cornflour
- pinch of salt
- 3 C milk
- 1 T butter
- 1 t vanilla essence
- ground cinnamon

Method

For the pastry case, mix all the dry ingredients together. Rub in the butter. Add the egg and milk and mix well. Place the pastry in the fridge for 1 hour. Press the dough into 2 pie dishes and bake blind for 10 minutes. Allow to cool. For the filling, beat the eggs and sugar; add the flour, cornflour and salt with 1 T milk. Mix well. Bring the rest of the milk and the butter to the boil, add the vanilla essence and remove from the heat. Add the egg mixture to the milk and stir constantly until the mixture thickens. Pour into the pastry cases. Sprinkle the tarts liberally with cinnamon.

Molasses and Fig Steamed Pudding

That Lyndall broke my special plate today. No pudding for her! We have visitors coming tomorrow so we must have plenty to eat at teatime. We will need 1 T butter, 1 T mutton fat, 1 C sugar, 2 eggs, 1 t bicarbonate of soda, 1 C milk, 2 C flour, salt, 1 C breadcrumbs and 1 lb figs. Cream the butter, fat and sugar; add the eggs, bicarbonate of soda and milk. Lastly add the flour, salt, breadcrumbs and figs. Put into a well-greased pudding mould. Place the mould onto a rack in a saucepan of boiling water. More than half of the pudding mould must be submerged during cooking. Steam for 1½ hours. Turn out and serve with molasses sauce. Molasses sauce: 2 T butter, 1 large C molasses, 2 eggs (well beaten), ½ t cinnamon, ½ C milk and a pinch of salt. Put butter and molasses on low heat but do not allow to boil. When melted together, add the eggs, cinnamon, milk and salt, increase the heat and stir until it thickens slightly. Pour the sauce over the pudding while both are hot. Serve with custard.

MODERN VERSION – Malva Pudding

Ingredients
- 1 C sugar
- 1 egg
- 1 D soft butter
- 3 T apricot jam
- 1 C flour
- 1 t bicarbonate of soda
- pinch of salt
- 1 C milk
- 2 t brown vinegar
- 2 t vanilla essence

Syrup
- 1 C cream
- ¼ C butter
- ½ C sugar
- ¼ C hot water

Method

Cream together the sugar, egg, butter and jam until pale yellow. Sift the dry ingredients together; mix the milk, vinegar and vanilla essence. Alternating, fold the dry ingredients and the milk mixture into the batter. Pour the mixture into a large, buttered pie dish. Bake at 180 °C for 45 minutes. Make sure it is firm in the middle. Heat the syrup ingredients together until the sugar has dissolved and pour over the pudding while it is still warm. Serve with cream or custard.

Waldo

Mutton

That is it! The sheep are gone and so are the maid and her husband. Otto can make good the loss – no mutton for them tonight! We are going to pickle the legs, even smoke one. After pickling we may roll the leg in sawdust and hang it for 2 to 3 days in the chimney, over wood smoke. The neck is used to make stew, perhaps an Irish stew, or cut into chops to be cooked over the open fire. And we mustn't forget to salt the ribs.

We usually de-bone and stuff one of the shoulders for dinner and salt the other one for later. The sheep tail is rendered for fat, which we use for cooking and making candles. The 'kaiings' are made into a crisp, salty snack, which I like to eat before I go to bed. The fat can also be used to make candles. The head and the trotters are boiled in a pot with seasoning. When ready, the tongue is removed and skinned, and everyone knows the trotters are mine!

Otto comes from Germany and loves brawn. Traditionally we place the tongue, plus any other meat we have, in a mould. Take some stock, place it in a pot with an onion, then add a little vinegar and some salt. (Don't forget, brawn needs to be slightly over salted.) Boil it down and pour over the tongue and meat in the mould. Cover and allow to set. Sometimes we turn it out the next day and slice as cold meat. I give the leftovers to the labourers to cook in a big stockpot with whatever vegetables they have.

Naartjie and Almond Cake
– my mother's recipe

I could sit on the stoep and have cake and tea all day, and remember the old days. Ingredients: juice of 1 naartjie, 8 eggs, 250 sweet almonds, 25 bitter almonds (if no bitter ones available, toast 25 sweet ones), ½ of the naartjie's peel, pounded, 1 lb sugar and ¼ lb flour. To obtain the juice of the naartjie, place the fruit in a cloth and squeeze. Mix the egg yolks, almonds, naartjie peel and sugar, add the egg whites beaten to a stiff froth, then fold in the flour and naartjie juice. Bake in a moderate oven for about 1½ hours.

MODERN VERSION

Ingredients

3 naartjies
6 eggs
1 C castor sugar
2 C ground almonds
¼ C sugar
little water
almonds for decoration

Method

Boil the naartjies in water for 2 hours. Allow to cool. When cool, remove all the pips. Liquidise the naartjies to form a pulp. Set aside. Beat the eggs and sugar until stiff and yellow. Fold in the ground almonds and naartjie pulp until well combined. Bake at 160 °C in a well greased, round 24 cm spring-form cake tin for 1 hour and 15 minutes. Before taking it out of the oven, check that the middle is set. While the cake is baking, put the sugar into a small pan with a little water, allow the sugar to dissolve, without stirring, until it caramelises. Drop in almonds and use for decoration on the cake.

Nasturtium Seeds – Pickled
– used to replace capers

I sent Lyndall and Em out to find the seeds today. That Lyndall would read all day if you let her. Pick the seeds while they are still green. Soak them in brine for 24 hours. Rinse well and allow them to soak in fresh water for another 6 hours. Dry with a soft cloth and pack them in glass bottles. Cover with spiced vinegar. Add 1 t sugar, ½ t salt, ½ D peppercorns, a little ginger and a couple of whole cloves, to each bottle. Cover immediately.

As capers are not readily available to us on the farm, nasturtium seeds are a good substitute.

Nasturtium Seed Sauce

A sauce can be made from the nasturtium seeds to be served with tongue.

Melt 1 C butter over a low heat. Add to it 3 T pickled nasturtium seeds, cut up into small pieces and add 1 T nasturtium juice. Stir well and allow to simmer gently until the flavours have combined.

These days we seem to overlook the nasturtium seed and focus more on eating their flowers and leaves in our salads.

Oat Biscuits
– the children's favourite

I don't believe in spoiling the children, but every now and then when they are good, I make these for them. Ingredients: 1½ lbs butter, 6 T treacle, 6 t bicarbonate of soda, 4 C flour, 10 C oatmeal, 5⅓ C sugar and 3 C coconut. Melt the butter and treacle, bring to the boil, add the bicarbonate of soda and mix well. Add the remaining ingredients. Form into small balls. Bake in the bread oven at a moderate heat till brown.

MODERN VERSION – a slightly different version, these would be the crunchies we find in the shops today.

Ingredients

⅔ C butter   2½ C raw oats
1½ T syrup   1⅓ C sugar
1 t bicarbonate of soda   ¾ C coconut
1 C flour

Method
Bring the butter and syrup to the boil; add the bicarbonate of soda and mix. Remove from the heat, add the syrup mixture to the dry ingredients and mix well. Press into a greased baking tray of 45 x 30 cm. Bake at 190 °C for 15 minutes. Cut into squares while hot. Remove from the pans when cool.

Ox wagon

Quick Onion Soup

This is a very useful recipe as the ingredients are all in the loft. If somebody arrives unexpectedly we can make it in 10 minutes. This is the soup Bonaparte greedily ate up on his first day on the farm. Grate 1 onion and 1 potato. Place in a pot with ½ C water and simmer gently for 5 minutes. Add 1 T butter, 1 T chopped parsley, 1 C milk, salt and pepper to taste. Simmer for a further 3 minutes and serve.

MODERN VERSION – Vichyssoise

Ingredients
4 leeks, chopped
1 medium onion, chopped
2 T butter
5 medium potatoes, peeled and chopped
4 C chicken stock
1 t salt
2 C milk
2 C cream + 1 C cream
chopped chives

Method
Fry the leeks and onion in the butter until they turn golden. Add the potatoes, chicken stock and salt and boil for 35–40 minutes. Liquidise and return the mixture to the heat, add 2 C milk and 2 C cream. Season to taste and bring to the boil. When cold, add the other cup of cream. Chill thoroughly. Serve with chopped chives on top. Have black pepper on hand for people to add if they wish.

Ovens

Indoor harth and bread oven

The earliest known man-made oven was the three-legged pot; it was used for baking, roasting and stewing. The 'Dutch' oven, on the other hand, was fashioned on the termite mound oven; it was either close to the house or accessible through a door on the side of the hearth. Even when metal stoves, utilising either wood or coal, were introduced, 'Dutch' ovens were still used, as the single stove could not cope with the baking demands of the farm.

Outdoor oven

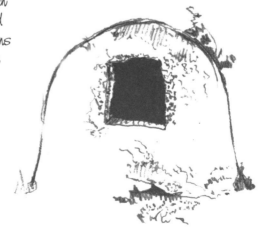

Ovens cont.
Termite Mounds

My mother, her mother and her mother's mother used these mounds to cook in. They are one of the oldest ovens.

If you are in the bush and in need of an oven, just make a hole in the side of a termite mound. Make a fire and when the heat is right, place the bread or meat into the mound, seal the hole and cook.

Termite mounds are very well insulated because they are made of clay. They are also very well ventilated because of all the tunnels. Any baking can be done in these ovens.

Snakebite remedy

Make sure you check termite mounds for snakes and monitor lizards before using them as an oven because lizards really like the mounds for their constant heat. One of my maids was bitten by a snake and we were taught that when somebody is bitten by a snake, you immediately put on a tight tourniquet above the bite and suck the poison out of the wound as quickly as possible. Clean the wound with ammonia and give the patient sulphuric acid - 20 drops in water every 3 hours. Sal Volatile can also be given every couple of hours. We have never lost anyone to a snakebite, thank the Lord!

Peach Mebos

I keep the peaches up in the loft so the children can't get to them, but Bonaparte saw Waldo sneaking up there the other night – he got a real hiding for it. Peel clingstone yellow peaches and boil in water until they are soft. Remove the pulp from the stone and put through a sieve. For every 1 C peaches add ½ C sugar. Put the peaches and sugar into a saucepan and boil, stirring all the time until the mixture becomes thick. Spread out about ½ inch thick on greased baking sheets. Allow to dry until it is no longer sticky – about 4 days. Cut into squares, roll in sugar and store in a wooden box. This recipe has stood the test of time, so there is no need for a modern version.

Peach Preserve

Peel and halve 4 lbs peaches (clingstone). Make syrup with 4 C sugar and 2 C water. (For every pound of fruit allow 2 C sugar and 1 C water.) Bring the syrup to the boil, drop in the peaches and cook until they are clear and tender. Pack them in jars that have been boiled for 15 minutes, cut side down. Fill the jars to the top with the syrup and seal immediately.

Brandied Peaches

We have so many peaches on the farm. I like to put them to good use in some brandy! They make a very nice pudding and the leftover brandy is good to use in my Christmas cake. Weigh the peaches and use the equivalent amount of brown sugar (for each cup of sugar use ½ C water); 18 firm ripe peaches, peeled; enough good brandy to fill the jars. Put the sugar and water into a deep pot, heat and allow the sugar to dissolve. Drop the peaches into the syrup, for about 10 minutes, until tender. Put the peaches into sterilised jars, pour the syrup over them allowing at least ¼ of a jar space for the brandy. Fill with brandy. Seal immediately. Allow to stand for at least 2 months before using.

Pickled Leg of Pork – ham

Bonaparte spends a lot of time down by the pigpen. I wonder what he is up to! I'll make him think of me when he eats pork tonight! Put the pickled pork into cold water and boil for 1½ hours. Pour off the water; add fresh water to the pot plus 6 whole cloves, 1 t allspice, 1 t ground nutmeg, a blade of mace, 1 t cinnamon and 4 chopped apples. Boil the leg for a further 20 minutes per pound. Remove from the water and skin. Score the fat in a diamond pattern. Rub the fat with 1 T mustard and 1 cup brown sugar. Place the leg in a roasting dish, use some of the syrup from the apricot preserve and put a few of the apricots in the dish with a dash of white wine. Place in a hot oven and cook until the sugar caramelises on the ham. Remove. Serve cold or hot. Serve with some of the gravy from the pan.

MODERN VERSION – from my friend Sheila

Ingredients
1 x 10 kg raw pickled and smoked ham
1 x 340 ml beer
1 T English mustard powder
1 C brown treacle sugar
1 x 410 g tin pineapple rings
8 glacé cherries
½ x 750 ml bottle white wine

Method
Place the ham and the beer into a large roasting pan. Cover with foil, sealing completely. Bake at 180 °C for 1 hour, then for another 25 minutes per kilo at 120 °C. Remove the skin. Score the fat, glaze with a mixture of hot English mustard and brown sugar. Place pineapple rings and cherries on top and secure with toothpicks. Use the juice from the pineapples and the white wine to baste. Remove when the sugar caramelises.

Potbrood – pot bread

Take two thirds of your plantjiebrood (yeast) (see page 99) and mix with enough flour to make a sloppy porridge mixture. Cover and allow to stand overnight. Add this to the following ingredients: 10 C coarse flour, 2 T salt and 2 T sugar – mix in well. Add enough warm water to make a moist dough. Knead the dough until it is elastic and does not stick to your fingers. Place back into the bowl, cover and keep in a warm place until it has doubled in volume. Beat it down and knead again. Now place into a greased cast iron pot. It may need two pots, depending on the size of the pot. Allow to double in size again, filling the pot. Make a hole in the ground and prepare your coals. When the dough has risen in the pot, pull the coals to the side and place the pot in the hole. Check the bread after 30 minutes and add coals if more heat is needed. Roosterkoek (see page 82) and potbrood are prepared the same way; the only difference is the cooking method.

Prickly Pear Leaf Soap

When Waldo isn't watching the sheep I send him out to pick the leaves, but I always have to remind him not to pick them when there is fruit on the leaves. That boy never listens. We make the soap when there is no fruit on the leaves. If there is fruit, the leaves are too lean. If you want to make white soap, peel the leaves. If the leaves are pale green you can remove the thorns and use. This will give you pale green soap. I always make sure that the girls scrub behind their ears. Ingredients: 28 lbs prickly pear leaves cut into quarters lengthwise, 14 lbs fat, 3¼ lbs. caustic soda and 6 quarts water.

cont.

Prickly Pear Leaf Soap cont.

Put the leaves, fat, caustic soda and water into a large pot. Boil, stirring constantly. After 15 minutes remove the veins of the leaves. Carry on boiling until the mixture looks like honey. To test, rub between two fingers. If it turns into hard fat it is ready. Line a box with a cloth, pour in the soap mixture, and cover with a second cloth. Allow to dry for 3 days. Cut the soap into bars and allow to dry for a further 3-4 days until completely dry.

Puff Pastry

Place ½ lb butter in a bowl of cold water. Work the butter in the water until it becomes smooth and waxy. Put the butter into a cloth and squeeze out any excess water. Sift 2 C flour and ½ t salt into a bowl. Add 1 T of the butter and work it into the dough with your fingers. Add cold water (about ½ C), gradually working it into the dough with your fingers, until the dough has the same consistency as the butter. Roll the dough out into a rectangular shape, about ¼ inch thick. Flatten the butter into a rectangular shape to fit into the middle third of the dough. Fold the upper third down and the lower third up. Seal the edges. Turn the dough so the edges face you. Roll out again. Repeat 3 times, making sure you seal the edges so that no air is lost, as this is what makes the pastry puff. Place in a cool place for ½ hour, then repeat with another 3 turns. Again place in a cool place. The dough must be cold when you use it. If making pies, roll out and place on a plate or pie dish. Prick the bottom and blind bake in a very hot oven at 450 °F. This pastry is ideal for tarts and sausage rolls.

MODERN VERSION

Ingredients
250 g butter
bowl of iced water
2 C flour
½ t salt
± ¾ C iced water

Method

Work the butter in a bowl of iced water with a wooden spoon until it is like a soft dough. Remove the butter from the water and dry. Wrap in wax paper and refrigerate until it is firm. Place the flour onto a work surface, add the salt and gradually work the water into the flour with your hands. Do not knead, as it will become too sticky. When the dough is firm, wrap it in wax paper and refrigerate for at least 30 minutes.

Place the dough on a floured work surface; roll it out into a rectangle. Form the butter into a rectangle that will fit into the middle third of the dough. Fold the top half of the dough down and the bottom half up. Press the edges together so no air can escape. Chill for another 30 minutes. Put the dough onto the floured work surface in the same position, roll into a rectangle and fold again. Repeat the last step. Place into the refrigerator for 20 minutes. Repeat again. You can now keep the pastry in the refrigerator for several days. Before using, roll into a rectangle and fold twice again. This sounds complicated, but it isn't. The effort is well worth it.

Pumpkin – Baked and Stuffed
– Riette Krige's recipe

I have invited Bonaparte to join us. I am making this lekker* baked pumpkin for dinner. Bonaparte will fall even more in love with me when he eats it. Ingredients: 1 small pumpkin, 2 T lard, salt, 2 large onions, 6 T lard, 2½ C breadcrumbs (dried in the oven), ½ t salt, black pepper, 1 t dried sage and 2 C cream. Cut the top off the pumpkin and remove the pips and fibres. Lard the inside of the pumpkin and salt lightly. Fry the onions in lard until soft. Stir in the crumbs and cook for a few minutes. Add the seasoning and cream. Use this mixture to fill up the pumpkin. Cover with the pumpkin lid. Place into a potjie and put enough coals underneath it to cook the pumpkin slowly for about 2 hours. *Afrikaans for nice/delicious/good

cont.

Pumpkin – Baked and Stuffed cont.

MODERN VERSION

Replace the lard with butter. Add courgettes and perhaps a few mushrooms. Grated Gruyère cheese would also be good; add a bay leaf on top. Bake at 180 °C for 2 hours.

Pumpkin Fritters

Place the pumpkin in a pot with the lid on and place in the oven. Do not add water – it will soften in its own juice. When soft, mash and allow to cool. Add flour to thicken the pumpkin so it has some form. Beat two eggs with a pinch of salt and add to the pumpkin. Heat some fat in a heavy-bottomed pan, put spoonfuls of pumpkin into the fat and fry until golden on both sides. Serve hot with cinnamon and sugar.

MODERN VERSION

Ingredients
2 C steamed pumpkin, mashed
2 eggs, beaten
¾ C flour

3 t baking powder
salt and pepper to taste
oil and butter for frying

Method
Mix all the ingredients together. Heat the oil and butter. Spoon the pumpkin into the pan and fry until golden brown on both sides. Place on brown paper to drain the fat. Sprinkle with cinnamon and sugar. This is a side dish that complements so many meat dishes.

Quail

Quail is very similar to pigeon. Otto used to shoot them in season from October to November, so they were usually fat enough. They are quite rich, so they definitely do not need larding or any rich stuffing. We wrap them in fig leaves, put them into a pot with a little white wine and allow them to simmer gently until cooked. Good served with an onion sauce. Brown 4 T lard or butter, add 2 T flour; when combined with the butter pour in ½ C stock. Add 1 C of finely chopped onions, and then add another 1½ C stock. Stir to make sure everything is combined. Allow to simmer gently until the onions are soft.

MODERN VERSION – from a friend in Graaf Reinet

Ingredients

4 quails
butter
flour, a little for rubbing
salt
black pepper
oil for frying
1 onion, finely chopped
3 cloves garlic, crushed
250 g streaky bacon, chopped
1 x 200 g punnet button mushrooms
3 C red wine mixed with stock
sliced julienne carrots – be generous, since this absorbs the richness
flour and butter mixed together to form a knob

Method

Rub the quails with a little butter, flour, salt and black pepper. In a pan heat a little oil and fry the quails until browned on all sides. Remove from the pan, then fry the onion, garlic, bacon and mushrooms. Return the quails to the pan. Pour in the wine and stock. Place the carrots on top and close the pan. Cook in a moderate oven at 160 °C for 2 to 3 hours. If the sauce needs thickening, add the knob of flour and butter. Serve with wild brown rice and a salad.

Queen's Pudding

Bonaparte is going to love this! He says he is related to Queen Victoria, you know. He says his nose is so red because where he comes from the redder your nose the higher you are! Ingredients: 12 thin slices bread and butter, 8 eggs, 8 C milk, 4 T sugar, 2 C peach jam and 4 more T of sugar. Cut the bread slices into four and put them into a buttered, flat-bottomed, ovenproof pan. Separate the eggs. Whisk the egg yolks, add the milk, then the sugar and mix together well. Pour the mixture over the bread. Allow to stand for 15 minutes, then put the pan into another pan containing water and bake in a moderate oven for 35 minutes. Make sure the custard is set. Remove from the oven and spread the jam on top. Beat the egg whites stiffly, fold in the rest of the sugar with a fork and spread the meringue on top of the jam. Bake again in a slightly cooler oven until the meringue has set and is slightly browned.

MODERN VERSION – Floating island – this is a lighter version.

Ingredients
CARAMEL
¾ C sugar   ¼ C water

MERINGUE
6 egg whites   1 t vanilla essence
¾ C sugar

Bonaparte

CUSTARD SAUCE
1 C milk   2 D sugar
1 C cream   1 D cornflour
4 egg yolks   1 t vanilla essence

Method
Spray an ovenproof bowl with non-stick cooking spray. Put the sugar and water into a small pan and heat. Allow the sugar to melt and form a caramel (do not stir). Pour the caramel into a bowl, coating the sides well. Allow to set.

Method cont.

To make the meringues, beat the egg whites well until they form peaks, then add the sugar, one spoon at a time, beating after each addition. The mixture will become stiff and glossy. Fold in the vanilla essence. Make sure the caramel is set before putting the meringue into the bowl. Press it down well to prevent bubbles. Place the bowl in a pan filled with water, making sure the water cannot get into the meringue. Bake at 140 °C for 30 minutes – make sure it is set before removing it from the oven. When it is cool, tip the meringue out onto a dish large and deep enough to hold the custard. Do not worry: as the meringue cools it will sink in the middle.

To make the custard, scald the milk and the cream in the top of a double boiler – do not let it boil. Beat the egg yolks and sugar until creamy and light, then slowly add the cornflour and vanilla, and beat until blended. Slowly add the scalded mixture to the egg yolks, beating continuously as you do so. Return this mixture to the double boiler and cook until thickened, stirring all the time with a wooden spoon. When cool, pour the custard around the meringue on the dish and lift the meringue slightly to allow the custard to spread beneath it.

Quince Jelly

The quince is a common tree and the fruit used to be as well known as the apple and the vine. It is not good to eat raw but because of its very high pectin content, it is excellent for jellies and jams.

I always make sure I have lots of this fruit. The aunties who come to visit love it. To get a clear jelly you must pare and peel the quinces. Cut up into small pieces and cover with water in a saucepan. Cook until the fruit is soft.

cont.

Quince Jelly cont.

Strain the liquid through a cloth. Allow ¾ lb sugar for every 1 lb juice. Heat the juice in a saucepan and when it boils, add the sugar. As soon as the sugar has dissolved, strain the liquid through a second cloth. Rinse the pot, return the strained liquid to the pot and allow to boil rapidly until it starts to thicken and when tested on a plate, turns to jelly. Never stir the jelly. Skim the liquid carefully during the boiling process. Fill hot, sterilised bottles and place in a wide pot of boiling water. Allow the bottles to remain in the water for 5 minutes. Remove the pot from the heat and leave the bottles in the hot water for a further 15 minutes. Remove from the water and allow to cool overnight before sealing. Cover with white paper dipped in brandy and seal immediately.

In the **MODERN VERSION** allow 1¾ C sugar for every 500 g fruit juice.

Quince Mebos

Ingredients: 5 lbs quinces and 5 lbs sugar. Peel and grate the quinces. Place in a saucepan with the sugar and boil, stirring all the time until it has a good thick consistency. Put the paste onto a baking sheet and bake in a moderate oven until dry. Cut into squares and coat in sugar. Pack in a wooden box.

MODERN VERSION

Ingredients
1 kg quinces, peeled and grated
5 C sugar
2 packets red jelly powder
sugar to coat

Method
Place the quinces and sugar in a heavy-bottomed pot over medium heat. Allow to boil for 20 minutes, stirring constantly. Remove from the heat and add the jelly powder. Pour the mixture onto a damp baking sheet and allow to set. Cut into squares and roll in sugar.

Roly Poly

My grandmother loved this! Ingredients: ¼ lb suet, ¾ lb flour, ½ t salt, 1 t bicarbonate of soda dissolved in a little cold water and enough water to make a stiff paste. Rub the fat into the flour and salt. Add the bicarbonate of soda and water; continue adding water until the dough is stiff. Roll this out and spread with quince jam. Roll up making sure the edges stick together. Dip a rectangular piece of muslin in hot water then flour. Wrap the roly poly in the cloth. Stitch up the sides of the cloth. Hang the roly poly in boiling water. Allow to boil for 3 hours. Remove from cloth and serve with hot custard.

MODERN VERSION – SWISS ROLL

Ingredients
¾ C flour
pinch of salt
1 t baking powder
3 eggs, separated

4 T castor sugar
½ t vanilla essence
apricot jam, warmed

Method
Sift together the flour, salt and baking powder. Beat the egg yolks and castor sugar until creamy. Add the vanilla. Gradually add the dry ingredients, mixing well. Stiffly beat the egg whites and fold into the mixture. Grease, flour and paper line a 45 x 30 cm baking sheet . Spread the mixture onto the tray. Bake at 240 °C for 7–10 minutes. Wet and wring out a dishcloth and lay it out. Place a piece of greaseproof paper on the towel and sprinkle with castor sugar. When the cake is ready, turn it out onto the prepared paper. Roll up quickly. Leave for a few minutes then open out and spread with the apricot jam. Roll up again in the cloth only. The cloth must be wider than the cake so that you can hang it over the edge of the table, holding the towel down with weights. This will ensure that the roll retains its shape. Leave until cold, then remove the covering and sprinkle with a little icing sugar using a sieve.

Roosterkoek

Since Otto died, Waldo just sits at his grave doing nothing. Shame, I suppose he is sad. You can always get another husband but you can never get another father! When my father died they could do nothing with me until I had eaten some roosterkoek and honey.

MODERN VERSION – given to me by Sandra and her chef, Dalene, at the Victoria Hotel in Cradock.

Ingredients
10 C bread flour
1 x 10 ml instant yeast
1 T salt
lukewarm water

Method
Mix together all the dry ingredients. Add enough lukewarm water to form a soft dough. Knead well, cover and allow to rise until double in size. Roll into a long sausage shape. Cut into pieces, making a square-shaped roll. You do not have to let them rise again, as they will rise while you cook them over the open coals. Place a rack about a brick high above hot coals. Cook the rolls, turning constantly, so they rise and brown. Delicious with potjiekos or butter and homemade jam.

Rusks

These are my best – sitting on the stoep with Bonaparte, dunking my rusks in my hot tea. Make a sponge as for bread using your plantjiebrood (yeast) (see page 99). Allow this to stand and rise the whole day. In the late afternoon melt 1 lb butter or lard and add to the sponge. Mix 1 lb sugar into 5 lbs flour, add the sponge and knead well. If too dry add more lukewarm water. Set aside to rise. Next day shape the buns and arrange them on a pan. When they have risen to twice their size, brush with egg or milk and bake in a very hot oven. When quite cold break each bun in half and dry in a cool oven. Do not cut them with a knife. Store in tins.

MODERN VERSION

Ingredients

2 C buttermilk
3 eggs, beaten
2 C butter
3 T honey
5¾ C wholewheat flour
1 C white flour
1 C either sunflower seeds,
   raisins or pecans or a mixture

3 C bran crunch
2 C oats
1¾ C sugar
1 t salt
1 t cream of tartar
1 t bicarbonate of soda
1½ t cinnamon

Method

Mix the buttermilk with the eggs, then add the butter and honey. Mix the dry ingredients then add the wet ingredients. Add water if the mixture is too dry. Grease a deep baking dish, put the mixture in and bake at 190 °C for 40 minutes. Cut into squares while still hot and in the dish, and dry in a cool oven for 6 hours. Store in an airtight container.

Waldo and Doss at Otto's grave.

Waldo with Doss

Sheep Tail Fat

Sheep tail fat is as delicious for us as it was for our forefathers. We use it for cooking, along with pork lard. We don't like to use the oil from the sheep's trotters, as we only get a little from that. We use the fat as a spread instead of butter. In fact, we actually prefer it to butter. Once the fat has been rendered from the tail we are left with the kaiings. This is just like crisp pork crackling. We serve it with a sprinkle of salt and it is a treat for everybody.

The kaiings would have been like a packet of crisps today. These days sheep tails are docked, but in the 1820s, especially in the False Bay area, a sheep tail could weigh anything from 6-30 lbs.

Short Pastry – rich

This pastry is good for jam tarts and fruit flans. Ingredients: ½ lb flour, 1 oz sugar, salt, 6 oz butter, yolk of 1 egg and water. Combine the dry ingredients. Rub in the butter with your fingers. Add the egg yolk and as little water as possible to form a stiff dough.

MODERN VERSION

Ingredients
2 C flour
¼ C castor sugar
pinch salt
¾ C butter
cold water

Method
Place the dry ingredients into a bowl. Rub in the butter Add as little cold water as possible to make a stiff dough. Wrap and keep in the fridge until needed.

Sour Cream Pastry

Ingredients

3 C flour
½ t salt

1 C butter
1 C sour cream

Method

Sift the flour and salt. Rub in the butter until it is like breadcrumbs. Add the sour cream and mix until firm. Knead until the dough forms a ball. Roll out, fold in thirds, and seal the edges. Repeat this twice more with the sealed edges facing you. Store in a cool place or in the fridge overnight. This pastry is excellent with any meaty pie, especially venison.

Springbok Leg – oven or potjie roasted

A herd of springbok came across the plain the other day so all the men on the farm rushed out to hunt. Lard the leg of springbok well with mutton fat. Cut incisions in the flesh and push the sheep fat in. To make the marinade, boil together for a few minutes 1 C vinegar, 3 C red wine, 4 T brown sugar, 4 whole cloves, 2 cinnamon sticks and a blade of mace. Allow it to cool and place the leg in. Allow the leg to marinade for 24 hours, turning frequently. Remove the leg from the marinade. Heat 4 T lard either in a heavy-bottomed roasting pan with a lid or in a potjie. Brown the leg on all sides, then remove. Add some cubed pork to the pan so that the springbok is not too dry. Brown it in the lard with 4 sliced onions. Return the leg to the pot, add 2 pints stock, salt and pepper and 4 T quince jelly; peel and slice 5 large potatoes, plain or sweet, and add to the top of the pot. Close and allow to cook gently, undisturbed for 3 hours. Remove the meat and carve. If the sauce is not thick enough, thicken with a little flour mixed to a paste with the pan juices. Return the meat to the pot and serve with the potatoes from the pot.

MODERN VERSION

Marinade

8 T brown vinegar
1 x 750 ml bottle red wine
4 T oil
4 T brown sugar
4 bay leaves
2 t black pepper corns
4 cloves
2 cinnamon sticks
1 t garlic, mashed

Heat all the ingredients together and boil for a few minutes. Allow to cool before using.

Ingredients

leg of springbok
250 g streaky bacon, sliced in small rectangles
4 T oil
4 large onions, chopped
1 T salt
black pepper
3 C beef stock
2 jars redcurrant jelly, or any sweet jelly
5 large potatoes, sliced (sweet or plain are equally as good)

Lard the leg of springbok with the bacon. Make incisions in the leg and press the bacon into the holes. Marinade the leg for at least 24 hours, turning the meat regularly. Remove the leg from the marinade. Put the oil in either a heavy-bottomed roasting pan with a lid or in a potjie. Brown the leg of springbok on all sides to seal. Remove the meat and brown the onions, then return the meat to the pot. Season; add the stock and the marinade. Bring to the boil, either on top of the stove or over the open fire. Stir in one jar of jelly. Place the sliced potatoes on the top and close.

cont.

Springbok Leg – oven or potjie roasted cont.

If using a potjie, you need to have a large amount of coals to brown the meat and the onions. Remove some of the coals so you have a more gentle fire and allow the meat to cook undisturbed for about 3 hours. When the meat is tender, carve it and serve with the pan juices and potatoes from the pot. If roasting in the oven, cook at 180 °C for about 3 hours until the meat is tender. At this point you can thicken the pan juices by making a paste with flour and some of the juices. Add this to the juices in the pot and stir until it thickens. It is a good idea to add cream at this point; it enhances the flavour. Serves 8–9 people. Serve with the second jar of jelly.

HINT – Place sliced bacon rectangles on greaseproof paper, and cover with a second sheet. Place in the deep freeze. This makes it easier to press the bacon into the incisions in the leg.

Stoning Raisins

The quickest and least messy way to stone raisins is to put them on a tray and place them in a cool oven until they are just hot through. Rub your hands with a little fat: open the raisins and the stones will come out easily. This is a good thing for the children to do to keep them out of mischief.

Suet crust

Good with savoury puddings. Ingredients: 1¼ C suet, 2 C flour, pinch of salt, 1 t bicarbonate of soda and water. Chop the suet finely (add a little of the flour – this makes it easier to chop). Add the rest of the flour, the salt and bicarbonate of soda. Mix, stirring in a little water at a time until you have a stiff dough. Place the dough on a floured surface and knead until smooth.

For the **MODERN VERSION** replace the bicarbonate of soda with baking powder.

Tongue

We never waste any part of the sheep. The tongue will be cooked with the whole head or pickled and boiled. I used to give the tongue to Otto for his work on the farm.

Apricot Sauce for Tongue

There are various sauces you can make for tongue:

Ingredients
¾ C water from the boiled tongue
1 C dried apricots
½ C brown sugar
3 T white vinegar

a handful of raisins
1 t hot mustard
½ t salt
1 T flour

Method
Place the water and apricots into a pot and simmer gently for 5 minutes. Add the sugar, vinegar, raisins, mustard and salt and simmer for a further 10 minutes. Take some of the water from the pot and make a paste with the flour. Remove the pot from the heat, stir in the paste and return to the heat, then stir until it thickens. Serve over the sliced tongue. A little cinnamon can be sprinkled over the tongue, but allow people to make that decision for themselves. A good sauce with tongue would be the Nasturtium Seed Sauce (see page 66).

Pickling a Tongue

Mix together 8 oz salt, 1 oz saltpetre, 3 oz coarse brown sugar, 10 whole cloves, 20 peppercorns and a quart of water. Rub all the ingredients well into the tongue. Place in the water. Allow to lie in the brine for at least a week; they can remain in the pickle for up to 2 weeks. The tongue can be smoked if preferred – pickle for 2 weeks, remove from the pickle and hang in a fireplace burning wood, not coal, for another week. To cook the tongue, follow the recipe on page 90.

cont.

Pickling a Tongue cont.

MODERN VERSION – Buy a cured tongue from your butcher.

Ingredients
1 cured tongue
2 large onions, sliced
3 carrots, sliced
black peppercorns

Method
Soak the tongue in water for an hour, drain and place in a heavy-bottomed pot. Add water to cover, the onions, carrots and peppercorns. Simmer slowly for about 2½ hours until the meat is tender. Remove from the water and remove the skin, then return to the water until cool.

Treacle Scones

4 oz flour, ¼ t cream of tartar, ¼ t bicarbonate of soda, ½ oz sugar, 1 oz butter, 1 T treacle, and some sour milk to mix. Sieve the dry ingredients into a basin. Rub in the butter with the tips of the fingers till like breadcrumbs. Mix the treacle with a little milk before adding it to the dry ingredients. Mix everything to a stiff dough. Knead well and roll out thickly. Cut into scones. Bake in a very hot oven for 7 to 10 minutes.

MODERN VERSION

Ingredients
⅓ C butter
2 C flour
2 t baking powder
1 C milk
¼ t salt

Method
Rub the butter into the flour. Stir in the remaining ingredients with a knife. Pat the dough into a rectangle about 2.5 cm thick. Cut into 12 scones and place on a floured baking sheet. Bake at 225 °C for 12 minutes. Serve hot with butter, jam or syrup and whipped cream.

Venison and Mutton Shank Stew

This we make on special occasions, like weddings. Who knows, mine might be next? I am going to sit up with Bonaparte any night now! Cooking the venison with the mutton enhances the flavour of both meats. Ingredients: 3 T lard, 3 lb springbok shanks, 3 lb mutton shanks, 3 thick slices ham, 2 large onions, use vegetables in season — perhaps parsnips, carrots, and a mixture of a few available herbs, 3 C red wine if available, 3 C stock, add more stock if wine is not available, 4 whole cloves and a blade of mace, salt, pepper and 3 T quince jelly. Heat the lard in a large pot or a three-leg potjie. Brown the shanks and ham. Remove from the pot and add the vegetables. Fry until soft and slightly brown. Put the meat back into the pot and add the remaining ingredients. If cooking in the oven, place in a moderate oven for 4 hours; turn the shanks about three times during the cooking process. The same timing would apply if you cook the meat in a potjie. Make sure your coals are not too hot — the meat must simmer gently. When the meat is ready to serve, remove from the bones, put back into the pot and check the seasoning. Thicken the juices with a few spoons of flour mixed with the pan juices to make a paste. Serve with mashed potatoes. Leftover meat from the stew can be used to make a delicious pie. Simply put into pie dish, cover the top with puff pastry or sour cream pastry, brushed with egg. Bake in a moderate oven for 30 minutes, until the pastry is golden brown. Serve with stewed dried fruit.

cont.

Venison and Mutton Shank Stew cont.

MODERN VERSION

LAMB SHANKS

Ingredients

salt
black pepper
8 lamb shanks
oil
2 onions, finely sliced
2 cloves garlic, mashed
1 bunch of celery, chopped
3 carrots, sliced

2 T sugar
1 x 750 ml bottle red wine
4 beef stock cubes, dissolved in 4 C water
4 sprigs rosemary, chopped
4 T butter
4 T flour

Method

Season the lamb shanks. Heat the oil in an ovenproof pot with a lid. Brown the shanks on all sides and remove from the pot. Add the onions, garlic, celery and carrots, and fry until soft. Return the shanks to the pot with the remaining ingredients, except the butter and flour.

Place the ovenproof pot into the oven and bake at 180 °C for 4 hours. Turn the shanks 2 or 3 times during the cooking process. When ready to serve, check the seasoning. Blend the butter and flour together and add to the pot to thicken the liquid. Serves 8 people.

Vetkoek

When we go visiting I always like to take vetkoek with me. Everyone knows mine are the best. Ingredients: 6 lb flour, ½ C oil, ½ C sugar, 1 t salt and 2 C milk. For the yeast take two thirds of the plantjiebrood (yeast mixture - see page 99). Follow the instructions to make your dough for rising. You will also need enough lukewarm water to make a sticky dough. Mix all the ingredients together. Knead until the dough becomes elastic and stretchy. Allow to rise to double the size. Press down again, knead and break into separate balls. Allow these to rise to double their size. Heat enough fat in a pot large enough to deep-fry the vetkoek. To test if the fat is ready: drop in a small piece of dough - if it floats to the top, it is ready. Put in a few vetkoek at a time, reduce the heat of the oil and fry until they are golden brown. These are good filled with jam or savoury mince, or simply to mop up the sauce from a good stew.

MODERN VERSION

Ingredients

7 C flour
3 t salt
2 t sugar
1 x 10g packet instant yeast
6 T butter, melted

2¼ C lukewarm water
oil for deep-frying
castor sugar
cinnamon
1 slab chocolate

cont.

Otto's violin

Vetkoek cont.

Method
Combine the flour, salt and sugar in a bowl. Add the yeast. Rub the melted butter into the dry ingredients. Add the water and mix well. This should give you a fairly stiff dough. It is a good idea to use half of the mixture to make doughnuts. To do so, add a little more flour – this will make the dough easier to cut in rings. If you have a kneading hook on your mixer, knead the dough for 5 minutes. If doing it by hand, knead the dough for 10 minutes. Cover the bowl and allow the mixture to rise for 20 minutes. Knead the dough again. Break half of the dough into 18 balls and cut the other half into doughnut rings. Cover and allow to rise for a further 30 minutes. Deep fry a few at a time in hot oil, hot enough to make the vetkoek float to the top. Turn only once, remove when golden brown.

When the doughnuts are cooked, roll in sugar mixed with cinnamon. The other option is to melt the chocolate and dip the doughnuts into it.

Umbrella Acacia

Watermelon Konfyt

We don't get watermelon very often but when we do it is a big day for all of us. Peel the watermelon, and remove the pink flesh from the inside, which is a real treat for everyone on a hot day. Prick the peel well with a fork. Cut it into shapes; simple wedges are fine. For every 4 lb peel use 1 T lime juice to 6 pints water. Soak the peel overnight in an earthenware jar in the limewater and weigh it down so it does not float to the top. The next day wash the peel thoroughly. Use 2 lb more sugar than peel and 2 C more water than sugar. For example: 5 lb peel, 7 lb sugar and 17½ C water. Bring the water to the boil and add the sugar; when it has dissolved, add the peel and simmer gently for about 3 hours until the peel becomes transparent and the syrup is thick. You can add bruised ginger and a cinnamon stick, which will add to the flavour.

The **MODERN VERSION** would be done in the same manner.

The calculations would be worded differently.
For every 2 kg peel use 1 T lime juice to 3 litres water.
Use 1 kg more sugar than peel and 2 C more water.
For example: 2.5 kg peel, 3.5 kg sugar and 17½ C water.

Wild Duck

Ingredients: 2 small ducks, salt and pepper, piece of pork fat, 2 onions, 1 parsnip, chicken stock, 4 cloves, 4 chopped sage leaves, juice of 1 lemon, butter and flour. Season the duck inside and out. Put the pork fat into a heavy-bottomed pot with a lid; fry the pork fat until there is enough fat in the pot to brown the ducks. Remove the lump of fat from the pot; brown the ducks on all sides, turning frequently. Remove the ducks and set aside. Slice the onions and parsnips and fry in the pot until tender and slightly brown. Return the ducks to the pot and add enough stock to cover them; add the cloves, chopped sage and a little lemon rind. Close the pot and simmer gently for about 2 to 3 hours until the duck is tender. Remove and carve into portions. Strain the pan juices, add a little butter mixed with flour to thicken, return the duck pieces to the pot and serve. This would be good with rice and some green beans.

MODERN VERSION

Ingredients

4 x 500 g wild ducks
2 t salt
ground black pepper
250 g bacon, diced
1 C chopped onion
½ C chopped celery
1½ C dry white wine
1½ C chicken stock

1 C water
2 small bay leaves
4 whole cloves
4 T butter
¼ C finely chopped spring onions
⅓ C flour
2 T orange rind, finely grated
¼ C brandy

Method

Season the duck with salt and pepper. Fry the bacon in an ovenproof saucepan with a lid and render all the fat. Discard the bacon keeping the fat. Brown the ducks in the bacon fat, turning frequently. Remove the ducks and set aside. Fry the onion and celery, add the wine, chicken stock, water, bay leaves and cloves. Return the ducks to the pan. Cover tightly and cook in the oven at 160 °C for 3–4 hours. Transfer the ducks to a platter. Keep warm. Strain the cooking liquid through a sieve, pressing down hard on the onion and celery. In a pan melt the butter and fry the spring onion. Add flour and mix well. Remove from the heat and gradually pour in the strained cooking liquid, then return to the heat and stir constantly until the sauce thickens. Reduce the heat and simmer for 5 minutes. Check the seasoning and stir in the orange peel. Warm the brandy, light it and pour flaming into the sauce. Remove the meat from the ducks and cut into bite-size pieces. Add the meat to the sauce and simmer over a low heat until warm.

Wors (Boerewors) - sausage

There is nothing like a good old barn dance and lekker braai. We love wors. Ingredients: 5 lb mutton, 5 lb pork, 2 lb sheep tail fat, ¼ C salt, 4 t pepper, ¾ C wine and vinegar mixed, 2 t cloves, 2 t nutmeg, 2 t mace, a mixture of available fresh herbs (a little mint is also good) and pork casings. Make sure you use good quality meat and remove all gristle. If a mincer is available, mince the meat three times, if not, pound the meat in a mortar. Add the sheep tail fat, finely cubed, to the meat mixture. Mix in all the other ingredients. Use your hands to make sure it is mixed together well. Fill the pork casings with the mixture. Hang the wors in a cool place for 2 to 3 days. This is a very good frying sausage. The wors can be hung in a cool place until dry, and then it keeps very well.

MODERN VERSION – given to me by Jonny at Northern Meat

Ingredients

1 kg veal
1 kg beef
1 kg lamb
1 clove garlic, mashed
1 t coriander

1 t barbeque spice
salt
black pepper
sausage casings

Method

Choose your meat carefully – 90% meat with 10% fat. Mince the veal, beef and lamb together. Mix in the rest of the ingredients and taste to make sure there are enough spices, salt and pepper. Fill the sausage casings. If making dry wors, add a little vinegar, as the meat will last longer.

Yeast – Plantjiebrood

This bread is made with a culture that is 'grown' in an earthenware jar with an airtight lid. It has been used as far back as the time of the ancient Egyptians. Water and flour are mixed in the jar with a little sugar and the yeast is 'caught' from the atmosphere. Half fill the earthenware jar with 4 C boiling water, then add 1 T sugar, and sprinkle 2 C of flour on top. Seal the jar, put in a warm place and allow to stand overnight. In the morning, add 1 C warm water, stir well, cover and allow to stand for a further 4 hours. The mixture should now be bubbling. Stir this mixture vigorously, pour two-thirds of the mixture off, and keep the remaining mixture in a cool place until you need it again. Add flour to the two-thirds and stir until you have a sloppy porridge-like mixture. Cover and leave to rise for 4 to 5 hours in summer or overnight in winter. The following morning add the sponge to the meal/flour and knead into dough for bread (This will be sufficient raising agent for about six loaves of bread.) Cover the dough and put in a warm place to rise. Once it has doubled in size, knead it again, form into loaves and place into pans to rise again. When the pans are full, bake the bread in a moderate oven for 45 to 60 minutes.

Yeast Potato – Soetsuurdeeg

In this method a medium-sized potato is washed and sliced and placed on the bottom of a medium-sized saucepan. Add two cups of warm water. Sprinkle a cup of flour gently over the surface of the water allowing the surface tension of the water to hold the flour. Cover with plenty of cloths and blankets, and keep warm, but not hot. Allow to 'grow' overnight. The following morning remove the potato and beat the mixture well. Add to the flour and knead to make bread as above.

N.B. This is tricky yeast to make and is not guaranteed.

Zebra Fillets

When a herd comes by, I let the labourers go out and hunt, and then they eat well for weeks. Zebras are just like donkeys so we do not eat the meat, only the labourers do. We only shoot zebra on the farm for their skins and their thick yellow fat, which we use for making soap. Bonaparte says he has never seen a zebra before!

MODERN USES OF ZEBRA

As a matter of fact, the flesh of the zebra is very good to eat, as long as you remove all the fat.

MODERN VERSION

Ingredients
lemon juice
2 zebra fillets
barbeque salt with no garlic
salt
black pepper

Method
Squeeze lemon juice onto the fillet, then season. Make a fire in your Weber kettle or open braai, and bank the coals to the side. Cook the meat in the middle over a high heat – it must be browned but pink in the middle. Remove from the heat and slice. The flavour of the meat is so good you do not even have to serve it with a sauce. A butcher friend told me zebra is the softest meat you will ever taste. The most important thing is to remove absolutely all the fat. He says zebra meat makes the best biltong (see page 14) – the secret is extra coriander and no garlic. It also makes excellent salami and Russian sausages. He says any of the cuts of the zebra will be extra tender.

Zoetkoekies – Sweet Biscuits

We have visitors coming tomorrow so I must make sure I have enough for teatime. Ingredients: 4 lbs flour, 3 lbs sugar, 3 t bicarbonate of soda, 1½ T ground cloves, 2 T cinnamon, finely pounded, ½ C ground almonds (optional), 1 T ground cloves, 1 lb butter, ½ lb sheep tail fat, 4 eggs and 1 tumbler dark wine (claret). Mix the dry ingredients and rub in the butter and fat. Add the eggs and wine and knead well. Roll out, cut into shapes and bake. Bake at 350 °F for 10 to 15 minutes if ⅛ inch thick and 15 to 20 minutes if ¼ inch thick. This recipe will make 150 biscuits depending on the thickness. They last well in an airtight container.

MODERN VERSION

Ingredients

6½ C flour
3¼ C brown sugar
1½ t bicarbonate of soda
½ T ground cloves
1 T cinnamon

¼ C ground almonds (optional)
1½ C butter
1 C red wine (claret)
2 eggs

Method

Mix the dry ingredients and rub in the butter. Add the wine and eggs. Knead well. Roll out, cut into shapes and bake at 180 °C. If the biscuits are 30 mm thick, bake for 10–15 minutes and if 60 mm thick, bake for 15–20 minutes. The spices can be changed according to taste. A bit of ginger or nutmeg can perhaps be added. The wine can also be replaced with milk.

Index

A
Alcohol overdose 7
Ant poison 7
Apple
    cake 8
    tart 9
Apricot
    chutney 10
    jam 47
    preserve 11
    sauce for tongue 89

B
Barley water 13
Bedsores – prevention and remedy 13
Biltong – home-cured 14
Biscuits
    basic 15
    gingernut 41
    oat 67
    sweet 101
Bobotie 16–17
Boerewors 98
Brawn 18
Bread 19
Bredie
    green bean 20
    pumpkin 20
    tomato 20–21
Burns 22
Butter – keeping cool and firm 22

C
Cabbage rissoles 23–24
Cake
    fruit 38
    naartjie and almond 65
Caper – nasturtium 66
Chicken pie 25
Constipation 26
Cough
    mixture 26
    remedy 26

Croup medicine 26
Crunchie 67
Curry sauce, francolin in cream 34–35
Custard
    soft for pouring 27
    tart 27–28

D
Dairy 29
Dandruff 29
Doughnuts 93–94
Duck, wild 96–97
Dumplings 29–30
    apple 30

E
Egg flip 32
Egg nog 32
Eggs, ostrich 31
    hard-boiled 32
    scrambled 31

F
Fig konfyt – green 33
Floating island 78–79
Francolin
    braised 34
    in cream curry sauce 34–35
Frikkadel 36–37
Fruit cake – Koosani 38

G
Ginger beer 39
Gingerbread 40
Gingerbread men 41
Gingernut biscuits 41
Guinea fowl 41
    in red wine 42

H
Ham – baked 72
Hare – roasted 43
Hints 44
Honey 44

I
Invalid
  care 45
  food 45
Irish stew 46

J
Jam
  apricot 47
  peach 48
  tart 49
  watermelon, konfyt 95

K
Kaaings 85
Koeksisters 51
Koesisters 51
Koosani – fruitcake 38
Krengler 52

L
Lamb
  shank stew 91–92
  leg of 53–54
Leg of
  lamb 53–54
  mutton 53–54
  springbok 86–87
Lemon
  curd 55
  juice 55
  peel preserve 56
  syrup 56
Light 57
Liver
  paté 58
  roll 58
Locusts – fried 58

M
Malva pudding 62
Marmalade
  dried peach and lemon 59
  rhubarb 60
Measures, weights and 6
Meatballs 36–37
Melk tart 61
Molasses and fig steamed pudding 62
Mutton 64
  leg of 53–54

N
Naartjie and almond cake 65
Nasturtium
  seeds – pickled 66
  seed sauce 66

O
Oat biscuits 67
Onion soup, quick 68
Ovens 69–70
Oven temperatures 5

P
Pastry
  puff 74–75
  short 85
  sour cream 86
Pavlova 27–28
Peaches – brandied 71
Peach
  jam 48
  mebos 71
  preserve 71
Pickled leg of pork – ham 72
Plantjiebrood – yeast 99
Potbrood – pot bread 73
Prickly pear leaf soap 73–74
Puff pastry 74–75
Pumpkin
  baked and stuffed 75–76
  fritters 76

Q
Quail 77
Queen's pudding 78–79
Quick onion soup 68
Quince
    jelly 79–80
    mebos 80

R
Roly poly 81
Roosterkoek 82
Rusks 83

S
Scones, treacle 90
Shank stew, venison and
    mutton 91–92
Sheep tail fat 85
Short pastry – rich 85
Snakebite remedy 70
Soetsuurdeeg – yeast potato 99
Sour cream pastry 86
Springbok leg – oven or potjie
    roasted 86–87
Steamed pudding, molasses
    and fig 62
Stoning raisins 88
Suet crust 88
Sweet biscuits 101
Swiss roll 81

T
Tart – jam 49
Temperatures 5
Termite mounds 70
Tomato sauce – basic 37
Tongue 89
    apricot sauce for 89
    pickling 89–90
Treacle scones 90

V
Venison and mutton shank
    stew 91–92
Vetkoek 93–94
Vichyssoise 68

W
Watermelon konfyt 95
Weights and measures 6
Wild duck 96–97
Wors (boerewors) – sausage 98

Y
Yeast – plantjiebrood 99
Yeast potato – soetsuurdeeg 99

Z
Zebra meat 100
Zebra fillets 100
Zoetekoekies – sweet biscuits 101